ALMOST A PSYCHOPATH

ALMOST A PSYCHOPATH

**Do I (or Does Someone I Know) Have a Problem
with Manipulation and Lack of Empathy?**

Ronald Schouten, MD, JD, Harvard Medical School

James Silver, JD

HAZELDEN®

Hazelden
Center City, Minnesota 55012
hazelden.org

Library of Congress Cataloging-in-Publication Data

Schouten, Ronald.
    Almost a psychopath : do I (or does someone I know) have a problem with manipulation and lack of empathy? / Ronald Schouten, James Silver.
        p. cm. — (The almost effect series)
    Includes bibliographical references.
    ISBN 978-1-61649-102-4
    1. Antisocial personality disorders—Case studies. 2. Psychopath—Case studies. I. Silver, Jim, 1963- II. Title.
    RC555.S36 2012
    616.85'82—dc23
                                                    2012004423

DSM–IV–TR Criteria reprinted with permission from the *Diagnostic and Statistical Manual of Mental Disorders*, Fourth Edition, Text Revision (copyright 2000, American Psychiatric Association).

Editor's notes:
The case examples in this book are drawn from media accounts or are composite examples based upon behaviors encountered in the authors' own professional experiences. None of the individuals described were patients or legal clients. The names and details have been changed to protect the privacy of the people involved.

This publication is not intended as a substitute for the advice of health care professionals.

17 16 15 14 13 12   2 3 4 5 6

Cover design by Teresa Jaeger Gedig
Interior design and typesetting by Kinne Design

Harvard Health Publications
HARVARD MEDICAL SCHOOL
Trusted advice for a healthier life

The Almost Effect™ **series** presents books written
by Harvard Medical School faculty and other
experts who offer guidance on common behavioral
and physical problems falling in the spectrum between
normal health and a full-blown medical condition.
These are the first publications to help general readers
recognize and address these problems.

❖

To my mother and my late father
R.S.

To my mother and the loving memory of my father
J.S.

contents

The Almost Effect

I once overheard a mother counseling her grown daughter to avoid dating a man she thought had a drinking problem. The daughter said, "Mom, he's not an alcoholic!" The mother quickly responded, "Well, maybe not, but he *almost* is."

Perhaps you've heard someone, referring to a boss or public figure, say, "I don't like that guy. He's *almost* a psychopath!"

Over the years, I've heard many variations on this theme. The medical literature currently recognizes many problems or syndromes that don't quite meet the standard definition of a medical condition. Although the medical literature has many examples of these syndromes, they are often not well known (except by doctors specializing in that particular area of medicine) or well described (except in highly technical medical research articles). They are what medical professionals often refer to as subclinical and, using the common parlance from the examples above, what we're calling *the almost effect*.

For example:

- Glucose intolerance may or may not always lead to the medical condition of diabetes, but it nonetheless increases your risk of getting diabetes—which then increases your risk of heart attacks, strokes, and many other illnesses.

- Sunburns, especially severe ones, may not always lead to skin cancer, but they always increase your risk of skin cancer, cause immediate pain, and may cause permanent cosmetic issues.

- Pre-hypertension may not always lead to hypertension (high blood pressure), but it increases your risk of getting hypertension, which then increases your risk of heart attacks, strokes, and other illnesses.

- Osteopenia signifies a minor loss of bone that may not always lead to the more significant bone loss called osteoporosis, but it still increases your risk of getting osteoporosis, which then increases your risk of having a pathologic fracture.

Diseases can develop slowly, producing milder symptoms for years before they become full-blown. If you recognize them early, before they become fully developed, and take relatively simple actions, you have a good chance of preventing them from turning into the full-blown disorder. In many instances there are steps you can try at home on your own; this is especially true with the mental and behavioral health disorders.

So, what exactly is the almost effect and why this book? *Almost a Psychopath* is one of a series of books by faculty members from Harvard Medical School and other experts. These books are the first to describe in everyday language how to recognize and what to do about some of the most common behavioral and emotional problems that fall within the continuum between normal and full-blown pathology. Since this concept is new and still evolving, we're proposing a new term, *the almost effect*, to describe problems characterized by the following criteria.

The problem

1. falls outside of normal behavior but falls short of meeting the criteria for a particular diagnosis (such as alcoholism, major depression, psychopathy, or substance dependence);

2. is currently causing identifiable issues for individuals and/or others in their lives;

3. may progress to the full-blown condition, meeting accepted diagnostic criteria, but even if it doesn't, still can cause significant suffering;

4. should respond to appropriate interventions when accurately identified.

The Almost Effect

Normal Feelings and Behaviors	The Almost Effect	Condition Meets Diagnostic Criteria for Full-Blown Pathology

All of the books in The Almost Effect™ series make a simple point: Each of these conditions occurs along a spectrum, with normal health and behavior at one end and the full-blown disorder at the other. Between these two extremes is where the almost effect lies. It is the point at which a person is experiencing real pain and suffering from a condition for which there are solutions—*if* the problem is recognized.

Recognizing the almost effect not only helps a person address real issues now, it also opens the door for change well in advance of the point at which the problem becomes severe. In short, recognizing the almost effect has two primary goals: (1) to alleviate pain and suffering now and (2) to prevent more serious problems later.

I am convinced these problems are causing tremendous suffering, and it is my hope that the science-based information in these books can help alleviate this suffering. Readers can find help in the practical self-assessments and advice offered here, and the current research and clinical expertise presented in the series can open opportunities for health care professionals to intervene more effectively.

I hope you find this book helpful. For information about other books in this series, visit www.TheAlmostEffect.com.

Julie Silver, MD
Assistant Professor, Harvard Medical School
Chief Editor of Books, Harvard Health Publications

acknowledgments

This book would not exist without the vision, creativity, and enthusiasm of Julie Silver, MD, chief editor of books at Harvard Health Publications, the editorial skills of Sid Farrar and the staff at the Hazelden Foundation, the hard work and timely advice of our literary agent Linda Konner, and the assistance and consistent good nature of Natalie Ramm at Harvard Health Publications. We offer our appreciation to Harvard University for its wonderful library resources, which allowed us to access the exciting work being done by the scientific community.

Ron thanks the psychiatry residents and fellows as well as the Harvard undergraduates he has been privileged to teach, for asking him the hard questions. He is grateful for the psychiatry residency training he received in the Harvard system at Massachusetts General Hospital and the Massachusetts Mental Health Center, where he was introduced to the complex and important interactions of law and medicine. He greatly appreciates the opportunity to pursue his interests provided by the MGH department of psychiatry and those who have led it since he began his psychiatry residency there: the late Thomas P. Hackett, MD, Ned Cassem, MD, SJ, and Jerry Rosenbaum, MD. He thanks his children, Schuyler and Alison, who in their unique ways have given him so much, as well as his mother, Charlotte Schouten, for always being there for him. And finally, he is indebted to Kimberly Glasgow for her support, love, and encouragement during this project.

Jim thanks all his teachers, from grammar school through law school, who showed him the virtue of making learning a lifelong pursuit.

Part 1

Minor Problems to Major Predators

1

Setting the Stage

One of our colleagues regularly opens his talks on malingering and deception by asking how many people in the audience have ever told a lie, even the smallest fabrication. Nearly every hand goes up. Then he asks how many have ever taken something that does not belong to them, no matter how insignificant, perhaps a paper clip or pen from work. Again, nearly every hand goes up. He then says, "It's nice to know that I'm speaking to an audience of liars and thieves." The audience laughs, because they recognize the truth of what he's saying: regardless of education, social status, or income, from time to time, our behavior is not always strictly moral or honest.

For most of us, though, anything more than telling a white lie or committing some other minimal misdeed makes us uneasy. We realize that there is something wrong with what we have done, are doing, or are contemplating. Whether it is blaming our own mistake on a co-worker, not telling the clerk when we are given too much change, or retaliating in-kind to that other driver who just cut us off, we know it isn't the right thing to do. If we do it anyway, because of a lack of impulse control at the moment or because we can somehow justify it, more often than not our conscience kicks in and we get that uncomfortable feeling that we know as guilt or shame.

Research has shown that we all rationalize both "good" and "bad" behavior. Social conventions that we learn from our parents and others, religious principles, and the potential psychological turmoil of a distressed conscience combine to deter most of us from routinely engaging in even relatively small transgressions that fall outside of communal norms, let alone more elaborate and harmful acts of deceit and aggression. Yet with all those factors helping us to behave as we should, it is still the case that everyone can have improper, even downright evil, thoughts and fantasies that they never act upon. And when it comes to cheating, taking advantage of others, infidelity, and the like, we have no shortage of examples of "good" people who stray from the straight and narrow.

The hazy and at times fluid boundary between "good" people and "bad" has been the subject of much study and discussion. Forensic psychiatrist Robert Simon captures the essence of this idea in the title of his 1996 book *Bad Men Do What Good Men Dream*. The famed Swiss psychiatrist Carl Jung theorized that everyone has a "Shadow" as part of the unconscious and that it contains repressed desires, weaknesses, and primitive animal instincts. Jung pointed out that the less the Shadow is acknowledged and "the less it is embodied in the individual's conscious life, the blacker and denser it is."[1] In other words, denying that we have such dark thoughts puts us at risk of being controlled by them. Others who study personality and its disorders (including psychopathy) have attributed these gaps in moral reasoning to *superego lacunae*—tiny holes in the superego, the part of us that tells us what is right and wrong.[2]

Research psychologists David DeSteno and Piercarlo Valdesolo, in their book *Out of Character*, explore the origins and consequences of our rigid notions of character, as well as the potential we all have for acting "out of character."[3] Through discussion of multiple experimental studies and examples drawn from recent headlines, they show that character is not as fixed as many of us might believe, and even those who profess the highest moral principles are not immune from often spectacular departures from the standards they expect others to follow, including former New York Governor Eliot Spitzer and political commentator Rush Limbaugh. The number of fundamentalist preachers and other religious leaders who also have had dramatic falls from grace are further evidence that even those who profess the strictest moral tenets can fail in their struggles with their own darker sides. Swiss psychoanalyst Adolf Guggenbühl-Craig suggests that some of the people most at risk for major transgressions of appropriate conduct are those who fight against their own darker impulses by adopting and proclaiming the strictest of moral principles. Unable to deal with their own emotions and moral ambiguity, they think in black and white and identify themselves with rigid moral codes and righteous causes, thus justifying their own behavior.[4]

Nevertheless, just as we recognize that some missteps are part of being human, we also know that there are people in this world who regularly and systematically do truly bad things, who seem to operate without the moral constraints experienced by the rest of us. These people seem different from everyone else—and in some very fundamental ways, they are. By virtue of the frequency and degree of their deviance from socially acceptable behavior, they are regarded as exhibiting *psychopathy:* a psychological condition that represents particular ways of behaving and viewing the world. They are psychopaths.

Psychopathy involves a major abnormality in how people interact with the world around them, characterized by a lack of empathy for other people's feelings as well as behaviors that are considered inappropriately deceitful, aggressive, and indifferent to the rights or feelings of others. The psychopath ignores social, legal, and moral standards of conduct in order to meet his or her own needs at the time, often ignoring potential long-term consequences in deference to immediate gains. The rest of us may violate those standards of behavior when our inherent sense of right is overpowered by factors that may include a sense of obligation to a group or cause or the ability to rationalize that it is okay "just this once"—allowing us to do something that we would ordinarily disapprove of for ourselves or others.

True psychopaths don't need to rationalize (although they will if their behavior is questioned). Antisocial behavior is their norm, not the exception. Of course, there are others who do not meet the full criteria for psychopathy and yet engage in heinous acts that most of us would turn away from in disgust and horror. If this were not the case, world history would not be full of tales of apparently normal people and societies committing acts of genocide such as the Holocaust and the mass killings in Rwanda.

But even routine patterns of deception or attempting to take advantage of others do not necessarily mean that a person is a psychopath; context and culture play important roles and are important factors to consider in assessing the nature of behavior. Take lying and conning others as an example. Generally speaking, in the United States, a person who relies on inflated representations and continually makes promises that he or she doesn't anticipate fulfilling is likely to be considered a psychopath (at least in casual terms)—unless the person is a politician stumping for votes.

Similarly, in a Middle Eastern bazaar, where exaggeration and haggling are an expected part of the experience, efforts to convince a tourist to visit a shop owned by "my cousin" and buy "the finest" carpets in the region at an inflated price are the first steps in a well-established, time-honored way of doing business. The hapless tourist who buys the rug at face value is the one with the problem and may even be insulting the merchant by refusing to bargain. On a more serious note, prisoners of war who intentionally and repeatedly deceive their captors to save their lives or the lives of others will be considered heroes, not psychopaths. The difference between these people and a true psychopath is that the psychopath will have exhibited a pattern of manipulating, conning, and perhaps violence in multiple settings—not just on the campaign trail or in the rug market—in a manner that is considered antisocial in his or her culture. No thought, no weighing of moral pros and cons is involved. Psychopaths are on automatic pilot, and their moral compass is either absent or, if present, always pointing in the direction of their self-interest.

In other words, perhaps the main difference between psychopaths and the rest of us is that they are not concerned about the difference between right and wrong. They *know* the difference;

they just don't care—their only concern is what's "right" for them. Psychopaths target the vulnerable, steal from the unwary, and deceive the weak (or, even more to their delight, the strong if they can get away with it), but no matter how much pain they cause with their deceit or whom they hurt, they don't experience the moral dilemma the rest of us do when we drift toward the darker side of behavior. While their ways can be violent and callous, their demeanor is often the opposite; psychopaths commonly have a glibness and charm that enables them to manipulate others and sometimes achieve success and apparent normalcy in their work and personal lives.

Even when their membership in this distinctive psychological category is discovered—perhaps when they are evaluated after having been charged with or convicted of a crime—it is unclear what to do with psychopaths, as current treatments for psychopathy have low to moderate rates of success.[5] This lack of success may be partly attributed to the psychopath's self-motivation for treatment, which is generally low. Why actively participate in treatment if you think nothing is wrong with you? Even when forced into treatment, psychopaths are likely to have only superficial and temporary motivation, lasting only as long as the treatment is mandated or until the psychopath can generate a reason to be excused.

While neither medications nor psychotherapy have consistently proven effective in treating psychopathy, a 2011 study by researchers at Emory University presents something of a good news–bad news story. The study found that after psychopaths with major depression began taking a standard antidepressant medication, they experienced a decrease in the very negative psychopathic traits of impulsivity and blaming others for their problems. On the other hand, this treatment appeared to lead to an increase in the socially adaptive psychopathic traits of glibness, social charm, and boldness in both their interpersonal and physical behaviors. In other words, they became less aggressive and reckless, but better able to manipulate and con others.[6] Interestingly, those personality changes were unrelated to changes in the symptoms of depression.

· · ·

For both of us (Ron Schouten and Jim Silver), psychopaths are part of our professional lives. Ron is a former attorney who left the practice of law to pursue a career in medicine. Planning to treat patients, he ended up devoting a good deal of his professional life to forensic psychiatry—the application of clinical psychiatry to legal matters. In his career, he has assessed men and women who were victims (and perpetrators) of child abuse, domestic violence, and other trauma, as well as offenders who murdered and assaulted multiple victims. Jim is a former federal prosecutor and criminal defense attorney who has tried cases and handled appeals on offenses spanning the gamut of illegal behavior from shoplifting to murder. We have seen our share of true, diagnosable psychopaths.

Nevertheless, we much more frequently find ourselves dealing with people who don't meet the current technical definition of a psychopath,* but who have more than the usual amount of difficulty following rules, fulfilling obligations, or understanding

---

* In this book, we will be using the conceptualization of psychopathy developed by Dr. Robert Hare and his colleagues for the professional tool known as the PCL–R: the Psychopathy Checklist–Revised. We will also refer to their work and that of others in extending the checklist's principles to noncriminal populations. We will describe that work in more detail in chapter 2.

how to treat others. They end up in our offices after the devil on one shoulder overpowers the angel on the other. The Shadow gains full control, however briefly, and those superego lacunae leave them blind to the implications and consequences of their actions. These people may get small things wrong regularly, leading to a string of problems in their personal or professional lives, or they may go off the rails in a dramatic and significant fashion that leads them to personal disaster or even the courthouse.

Whether because of the nature of their behavior—simply beyond what most of us can comfortably ignore—or because they violate social or legal norms so frequently, these people live their lives somewhere between the boundaries of common-place "not-so-bad" behavior and psychopathy. In that balancing of influences, their calculations more commonly lead them toward behaviors that most of us would find offensive and contrary to social norms. They are "almost psychopaths" because they exhibit some of the behaviors and attitudes of psychopathy but not to the extent that they meet the current formal criteria. In medicine, we refer to this as a *subclinical* disorder or *subsyndromal* condition.

We believe that all too often, those whose behaviors make them almost psychopaths are not recognized for what and who they are—subclinical psychopaths with problematic behaviors and attitudes that should be addressed before they cause more harm to others and themselves. We've written this book to help you and those you care about identify and deal with the almost psychopaths in your lives and to tell you that, unlike with a true psychopath, in many cases there *are* things that can be done to help address the behavior of an almost psychopath.

SETTING THE STAGE ❖

Since you've picked up this book, you probably at least suspect you have come into contact with an almost psychopath. They are spouses, co-workers, bosses, neighbors, political leaders, and, some people may wonder, perhaps themselves. On the surface at least, like true psychopaths, many almost psychopaths appear to live normal lives and have solid relationships at home and work. Yet, somehow, something is off. You've met these almost psychopaths, whether or not you knew it at the time, and after the fact have ended up scratching your head. "What was *that* about?"

We will offer some insights into what *that* was (and is) about. Drawing on scientific research and our own experiences, we describe the behavior, attitudes, and characteristics of almost psychopaths so that you can recognize them for what they are. Our case examples are drawn from real life, but except where noted, we have changed identifying characteristics, including names, to protect the privacy of those involved. For some examples, we've even combined aspects of different real cases in order to make specific points, as well as to further obscure the identities of these real-life characters.

Ultimately, this book is not about labels, as attractive as they may be for helping us organize our thinking about the world. Rather, it's meant to shed light on certain complexities of human behavior to encourage situational awareness. Our goals are to help you make sense of interactions you've had with almost psychopaths in the past and provide strategies for dealing with them in the present and future. And for those who recognize some of these concerning behaviors in themselves or who think they might be almost psychopaths, we describe the practical help that is available to help you understand and change your behavior and improve your life and the lives of those around you.

2

What Is a Psychopath?

Since we are going to be telling you about almost psychopaths, we first need to show you what they *almost* are. We begin with the story of a true psychopath.

Bill

Bill was the shipping and receiving clerk at a medium-size, family-owned business. Physically fit, good-looking, charming, and a military veteran, he was an easy hiring decision for the head of Human Resources. Bill initially was a good worker and ingratiated himself with his superiors, who felt that he had a real chance to work his way up in the business. His relationship with peers went less smoothly; they complained that he was irritable, even threatening, when they brought up shipping and receiving problems. One time, when questioned about an error he had made, Bill threw a handcart across the loading dock. He was active in the local gun club, and the office gossip was that Bill carried a loaded shotgun in the trunk of his car.

Even though weapons were prohibited on company premises, no one confronted him on this issue. His bullying behavior, coupled with the rumor about the shotgun, intimidated many of his co-workers.

Bill was interested in Amy, one of the company's administrative assistants, with whom he had gone to high school. He asked her out on a date, telling her how he had been attracted to her back then and had always thought she was the most beautiful girl in school. Amy politely declined, explaining that she had just broken up with someone and was not yet ready to date. Bill tried to persuade her to change her mind, and just to end the conversation, Amy agreed that he could ask her again at some time in the future. With any luck, she thought, he'll forget and get interested in someone else. A week later, he repeated his invitation, and Amy turned him down a bit more directly. That seemed to work. Bill stopped talking to her.

Instead, he looked up Amy's best friend from high school, Sara, and asked *her* out. He told Sara that he had always been attracted to her and thought she had been the most beautiful girl in school—just what he had said to Amy. Sara agreed to go out with him. On their date, Bill persuaded Sara to pose for some suggestive photographs. The next day, he wrote lewd captions for the photos, posted them on his Facebook page, and sent the link to Amy.

Six weeks after his last request for a date, Bill called Amy and told her there was a package in the mailroom that he thought might be for her and asked her to come down to identify it. Amy was wary, especially after the Facebook episode. She just had a feeling that there was something a bit odd about Bill. But he had always been polite to her, and she eventually decided that she was just being foolish. And, after all, they were at work. What could really happen?

Amy should have trusted her first instinct. There was no package. Bill had just learned that Amy had gone on a date with one of the middle managers of the company. When Amy walked into the mailroom, Bill slammed the door behind her. Enraged that she would go out with someone else after turning him down, he screamed at her never to lie to him or disrespect him again. Out of control with anger, he punched his fist through the wall. Amy managed to get to the door and flee upstairs. She went directly to the Human Resources office and reported what had happened.

Bill was called in to meet with the Human Resources director and the company's regional vice president, where he denied Amy's story, accusing her of exaggerating. When told that there had been employees outside the mailroom who had heard the noise and saw Amy run out in tears, he accused them of also exaggerating or misinterpreting things. "Sure," he said, "there was some pretty loud talking going on, but I was just trying to calm Amy down. She was upset because she found out that I went out with her best friend from high school." Lowering his voice as if he were speaking confidentially, he said, "She's a little jealous."

Management had no choice but to suspend Bill from work, pending a fitness-for-duty evaluation and violence risk assessment that included a background check and an interview with a psychiatrist retained for this purpose by the company. The thorough review of Bill's past uncovered a disturbing history: a restraining order taken out by an ex-fiancée, arrests for reckless driving, breaking and entering, two charges of assault and battery, and even allegations of check forgery and credit-card theft. It was also clear that since leaving the service, Bill had never owned or rented his own home, instead living with his mother and then various girlfriends. The military history he had listed on his employment application included inconsistencies about dates, places of service, and claimed ranks.

At the interview, Bill worked hard to ingratiate himself with the psychiatrist, complimenting him on his office, suit, education, and experience, and he seemed to be genuinely enjoying himself. He confided that he had searched the doctor's name online and expressed satisfaction that such a top expert in the field was evaluating him. He said that he was "really looking forward" to the doctor's opinion and hoped he could help "straighten out" the HR director and clear up this misunderstanding. Warned that their conversation would not be confidential, Bill assured the doctor that he had nothing to hide and would be completely honest, saying, "My life is an open book." Seeing the evaluator's diplomas on the wall, Bill bragged about his own academic prowess, explaining that he dropped out of high school due to boredom rather than pursue the college scholarship he was sure he would have received. He was downright chatty and readily acknowledged having had some problems with the law as an adolescent—all the result of misunderstandings, he assured the doctor—and having been in a youth detention facility prior to joining the military. Questioned about his military service, Bill claimed that he had been in combat on numerous occasions and had been sent on dangerous, secret missions that he was not allowed to discuss. In fact, the doctor knew that Bill had never been deployed overseas and had spent his entire military service maintaining equipment at a base in the United States. Bill told the doctor that he planned to work in his current job for only another few years and, having earned his general equivalency diploma while in the youth detention facility, was planning to go to college to become a doctor or lawyer, or both.

To prove his intelligence, Bill bragged about his ability to convince people, especially women, to do whatever he wanted. Questioned about his dating history, he proudly described having had relationships with multiple women—some at the same time—and being supported by several of them. Asked why he had had so many relationships, Bill matter-of-factly stated that he quickly got bored with these women, and most of them were not good enough for him, anyway. He reported that he was the father of two children, but readily—even proudly—admitted that he had claimed they were not his in order to avoid paying child support. When asked if he had ever been depressed, Bill responded yes, but was unable to describe what it felt like. While he said he was "very depressed" at times, usually over unfair treatment by others and their inability to understand him, he also described himself as a free spirit: "I do what I want, when I want."

When the conversation turned to the mailroom incident, Bill insisted that he had done nothing wrong. Asked how he thought Amy felt when he had closed the door behind her, screamed at her, and punched his fist through the wall, his only response was "I don't know." Encouraged to speculate, Bill eventually said, "I guess she could have been scared. But she shouldn't have pissed me off."

True Psychopaths

Bill is obviously not your average person with a few quirks. But why is he a psychopath as opposed to, say, an obnoxious guy with an anger management problem? The answer to that question lies in understanding what a psychopath is, how a psychopath is different from the rest of us, and the current measures that mental health professionals use to identify a psychopath.

What Is Psychopathy?

Psychopathy is a psychological condition in which the individual shows a profound lack of empathy for the feelings of others, a willingness to engage in immoral and antisocial behavior for short-term gains, and extreme egocentricity. Psychopaths do not have the fear response experienced by most of us to the potential negative consequences of criminal or risky behavior and are relatively insensitive to punishment. They tend not to be deterred from their self-serving behaviors by criminal or social penalties. In conjunction with their unfeeling and incessant drive to take care of themselves, psychopaths are predators, and anyone who can feed their need at the moment is potential prey.

Psychopaths are at increased risk of engaging in both *reactive* and *instrumental aggression*. Instrumental aggression (sometimes called *proactive* or *predatory aggression*) is planned, controlled, and purposeful, and is used for a particular aim—for example, to get drugs or sex, or just to establish dominance. The primary goal is not necessarily to injure others but simply to obtain the desired outcome. This isn't aggression that arises from an emotional reaction; it's the calculated use of aggression as a tool. Reactive aggression, on the other hand, is much more impulsive and emotion driven and arises from a perceived threat or attack or uncontrolled anger. The two types of aggression, instrumental and reactive, are not mutually exclusive. People can and do engage in both. The mob hit man may commit murder as part of his job but, like others, can experience road rage after a bad day at work. The point is that the reliance on instrumental aggression to get what they want is one of the unsettling things that distinguishes some psychopaths from the general population.

Worse, psychopaths are often superficially charming and glib; they are frequently able to take advantage of others because they know that acting genuinely friendly and helpful can be a useful strategy for getting what they want. While violence may be an option, a psychopath is just as willing to use a well-timed compliment, a subtle misstatement of the truth, or an exaggerated apology to achieve his or her self-serving goals. To a psychopath, a punch in the face and a lie hidden behind a friendly smile are merely separate tools to be employed as dictated by circumstances. The bottom line: psychopaths can be dangerous even as they outwardly present a pleasant and welcoming demeanor.

Are the Brains of Psychopaths Different?

Although various theories exist, there is no definitive answer as to what makes someone a psychopath. To summarize the research to date, psychopathy is the product of both nature and nurture—it is the result of the interaction of complex biological and social risk factors. The biological component includes findings of actual differences in the brains of psychopaths, especially in the regions associated with the formation of moral and socially responsible behaviors. Current neuroscience studies are leading researchers to conclude that psychopaths may not experience emotions that are thought to regulate moral and socially appropriate behavior. And there is evidence that these biological traits can be genetically transmitted.[7]

Researchers are using sophisticated brain imaging tests such as functional magnetic resonance imaging (fMRI)—basically, a "real-time" brain scan—to evaluate how psychopaths' brains may differ physiologically from those of people who exhibit normal behavior.[8] Some studies suggest that a dysfunctional amygdala in psychopaths leads to their characteristic lack of empathy.[9] The amygdala is part of the brain's limbic system that is involved in the regulation of emotions and nonconscious reactions, such as the fight-or-flight response, as well as memory. One theory is that structural and functional abnormalities in the amygdalae (one amygdala in each hemisphere of the brain) result in difficulties with emotional learning; psychopaths don't process emotional stimuli (such as distress in others) the way nonpsychopaths do.

One specific way that psychopaths may not process emotional stimuli as nonpsychopaths do was highlighted in research on how people react to facial expressions. In a study published in 2006 in the *British Journal of Psychiatry*, researchers used fMRI to examine how the brains of psychopaths and a control group responded when shown photographs of people with fearful faces, happy faces, and neutral faces.[10]

When viewing fearful or happy faces, the psychopath group had significantly less activation than did the control group in the two areas of the brain known to be stimulated when visually analyzing faces and when processing emotional (in contrast to neutral) faces. Interestingly, the type of expression viewed changed the response of the psychopaths. When viewing happy faces, *both* the control group and the psychopath group showed an increase in brain activity, although the increase in the psychopath group was measurably smaller. While the control group showed an increase in brain activity when viewing *fearful* faces, the psychopathic group reacted to the same images with an actual *decrease* in one of the two areas of the brain that processes facial expressions.

This is a small study with only male participants: six in the psychopathy group and nine in the control group. It nonetheless suggests that psychopaths process happy facial expressions much like others do (although with a more muted response) but that they process fearful expressions in a distinct way. These findings are supported by results of multiple other studies, including a 2008 study by German and Italian researchers that compared the way female psychopaths categorized emotional expressions. The subjects for this study were psychopathic and nonpsychopathic patients at a high-security forensic hospital in Italy, all of whom had been convicted of physical assault or homicide. A group of nonpsychopathic women was used for comparison. The study showed that of the three groups, the psychopaths performed the worst at recognizing sad expressions, gave less positive ratings to happy faces, and responded less to angry faces.[11] Taken together, these and multiple other studies indicate that psychopaths have a markedly different way of reacting to expressions of emotion. This provides an important clue as to why psychopaths do not appear troubled by causing distress in others or committing acts of violence, and may, in part, explain their overall lack of empathy.

. . .

Aside from processing emotional stimuli differently, the brains of psychopaths may help explain other facets of their person-

Wired for Pleasure?

Although much attention has been paid to the deficits that mark psychopathy (a lack of empathy, the absence of fear, and so on), there has also been interest in something psychopaths may have quite a lot of—a drive for rewards. In 2010, researchers at Vanderbilt University published results of a study that found an excessively active reward system in the brains of psychopaths—a finding that may help explain their characteristic traits of impulsivity and desire to take risks.

Volunteers were given personality tests to measure their psychopathic tendencies. Then researchers conducted two experiments while monitoring the volunteers' brain activity. In the first experiment, volunteers were given amphetamine—commonly known as speed—while a PET scan (positron emission tomography) measured the resulting release of dopamine, the neurotransmitter associated with reward and other brain functions. The conclusion? Those with strong psychopathy traits released nearly four times as much dopamine as those who had lower scores on the psychopathy scale. In the second experiment, using fMRI, researchers scanned the brains of the volunteers who were asked to perform a task in return for payment. The area of the brain associated with dopamine rewards (the nucleus accumbens) was much more active in those with high psychopathy scores than in the other volunteers.[12] It appears that the draw of rewards is more powerful for psychopaths than for the rest of the population, and the power of this draw may simply override any concern they may have for the consequences of their actions or the needs of others.

alities and behaviors. There is evidence of differences between the brains of successful and unsuccessful psychopaths; that is, those who evade detection and punishment versus those who end up getting caught and even incarcerated. This suggests that unsuccessful psychopaths have more problems with impaired decision making and poor behavioral controls, making them more likely to get caught.[13]

Psychopathy Is Not the Same Thing as Psychosis

It's important not to confuse psychopathy with *psychosis*, a psychiatric condition in which the person is out of touch with reality. A person who is psychotic might experience hallucinations (usually hearing or seeing things that aren't there, or sometimes hallucinations of smells, taste, or being touched) or delusions (there are many types, but all are basically false beliefs firmly held even in the face of evidence to the contrary). There are a variety of psychotic disorders, including schizophrenia, schizoaffective disorder, and delusional disorder. Psychotic symptoms can also occur in mood disorders like major depression or bipolar disorder (formerly called manic-depressive illness) and can develop with some medical or neurological conditions.

People who are psychotic do not necessarily lack compassion and empathy for others; any immoral or antisocial behaviors on their part are more likely the result of their difficulty in assessing reality than their lack of a moral compass. (That said, individuals with psychotic disorders can also be psychopaths—what one of our colleagues has referred to as *schizopaths*.)

Rather than being delusional or having difficulty perceiving reality, psychopaths know exactly what they are doing. While it might be preferable to assume that people who systematically commit unprincipled acts somehow just aren't aware of the harm they are causing, the reality is that psychopaths simply don't care whether they humiliate or injure others.

Psychopathy Is Not Synonymous with Criminality

Of course, given their proclivity for ignoring social norms and laws, quite a few psychopaths find their way into the criminal justice system, some spending significant portions of their lives incarcerated. Nevertheless, not all psychopaths are violent or serious criminals. In fact, most psychopaths manage to avoid involvement with the criminal justice system. Either their transgressions of social norms, while destructive and painful to those involved, do not rise to the level of criminal activity, or they are never apprehended by the police for the crimes they do commit.

While true psychopaths share certain behavioral and emotional attributes, they are not all identical, and they exhibit these various characteristics to a greater or lesser degree. Some psychopaths can control their self-serving behaviors so they remain (perhaps just barely) within the bounds of legal behavior, not because to do otherwise would be "wrong," but because being caught would unduly interfere with their efforts to get what they want. In some circumstances, psychopathic traits may actually *help* an individual become a well-regarded (although not necessarily well-liked) member of society. A superficially charming and engaging personality combined with a ruthless willingness to "do whatever it takes to get the job done" can be extremely useful in a high-stakes, pressure-filled environment. There is evidence that a combination of some of the psychopathic traits, certain characteristics of Machiavellianism (manipulating others for personal advantage) and narcissism, are found in some individuals who are skilled at obtaining positions of power and influence in the corporate and political worlds. These three characteristics, in combination, have been labeled the Dark Triad.[14]

While not all psychopaths end up behind bars, psychopaths *are* overrepresented in the prison population. They make up just 1 percent of the general population, but as many as 15 percent of female and 25 to 30 percent of male prison inmates meet the widely accepted definition of psychopathy.[15] Of course, this also means that the vast majority of those serving prison sentences are *not* psychopaths.

Nevertheless, psychopaths differ from the general incarcerated population in significant ways. Psychopaths who are imprisoned have committed more crimes and committed a wider range of crimes than the average prisoner.[16] They are also generally more violent during the commission of crimes than are other offenders.[17] As previously noted, psychopaths are more likely to employ instrumental aggression than nonpsychopaths who commit similar crimes; a 2002 study found that murderers who were psychopathic were significantly more likely to have committed premeditated (planned) murder than murderers who were not psychopathic, who were more likely to have killed in "the heat of passion."[18]

Psychopaths also tend to be more criminally active throughout much of their life span than are other offenders,[19] and when granted parole or some form of mandatory supervision, psychopaths are more likely to violate the conditions of their release and end up back in jail and prison than are nonpsychopaths.[20] They do not show reduced rates of reoffending in response to therapy, and they are up to four times as likely to reoffend by committing a crime of violence in comparison to offenders who are not psychopathic.[21]

A Dead Giveaway

We all have control over most of the words we choose when we speak—nouns, verbs, adjectives, and so on—and these words account for most of what we say. But we have less conscious control over many other words we use, and the tense in which we speak. Scientists believe that by examining the *unconscious* part of our verbal communication, they can gain insights into our psychological state. It turns out that the way psychopaths talk about their crimes is very revealing.

In a study published in 2011, researchers interviewed fifty-two convicted murderers, fourteen of whom were psychopaths, and asked them to talk in detail about their crimes. The researchers transcribed the interviews and then used a computer program to analyze the content of the murderers' speech.[22] The analysis revealed that when the psychopaths discussed their murders, they used a greater number of cause-and-effect words such as *because* and *so that* (suggesting a rational scheme) than do murderers who are not psychopaths. Murderers who are psychopaths also speak more in the past tense, possibly indicating a psychological detachment from their actions. Interestingly, the psychopathic murderers used almost twice as many words related to their own specific needs—food, money, sex—than did the murderers who are not psychopathic, who spoke more about family and spirituality in the wake of their crimes. These findings support the idea that at least some psychopaths view aggression and violence as tools to be used in the pursuit of their selfish goals.

Psychopathy Is Not Antisocial Personality Disorder

While the term *psychopathy* is generally accepted in the mental health community today, that has not always been the case, and there are now two schools of thought about the proper diagnostic term for people who persistently engage in socially inappropriate and illegal behavior. Generally speaking, one school of thought emphasizes consideration of both the person's behavior *and* emotional state (and uses the term *psychopathy*), while the competing view believes that assessing emotional state is too subjective and that the main consideration must be behaviors, which can be objectively measured. (This group uses the term *antisocial personality disorder* to describe these behaviors.)

The conflict between these two overarching views can be seen in the history of the primary diagnostic manual used by mental health professionals. In 1952, the American Psychiatric Society published the *Diagnostic and Statistical Manual of Mental Disorders (DSM)*. The manual was designed to present a standardized way to diagnose mental disorders. Each disorder listed in the *DSM* had a specific set of criteria that a person would have to meet to be diagnosed with that condition. The 1952 manual (known as *DSM–I*, as other editions followed) did *not* list psychopathy as a disorder. Instead, it contained a diagnosis of Sociopathic Personality Disturbance, with subcategories of Antisocial Reaction, Dissocial Reaction, Sexual Deviations, and Addiction. (The term *reaction* comes from the psychoanalytic theory that mental illness is the result of the mind's reaction to some earlier life event.) Nevertheless, the description of Antisocial Reaction was almost the same as the description of psychopathy used then. In the next edition of the *DSM*, Sociopathic Personality Disturbance was replaced by the diagnosis of Antisocial Personality, a diagnosis still similar in description to psychopathy.

The shift toward a diagnosis based largely on behaviors came when the *DSM–III* was published in 1980, followed by its 1987 revision, the *DSM–III–R*. In this version, a diagnosis of Antisocial Personality Disorder required evidence of antisocial behavior before age fifteen and focused on repeated acts that included lying, stealing, and getting arrested. This same approach was used in the current version of the manual, the *DSM–IV–TR* (with "TR" standing for text revision).[†] The diagnostic criteria remained unchanged from the previous version, but the explanatory text had been altered somewhat. In fact, as we will discuss shortly, there remains a significant difference between antisocial personality disorder and psychopathy, as the term is currently used.

The diagnostic pendulum has begun to swing back toward including emotional state as part of the diagnostic criteria. *DSM–V*, scheduled for publication in 2013, is expected to have a revised approach to personality disorders, including a category called "Antisocial/Psychopathic" that takes into account internal emotional state and other characteristics used to define psychopathy. (See appendix A for more on antisocial personality disorder.) Despite the controversy over the appropriate diagnostic criteria, there is a general consensus that *psychopathy*

---

† Throughout this book we will refer to various diagnostic criteria listed in the *DSM–IV–TR*, the American Psychiatric Association's *Diagnostic and Statistical Manual of Mental Disorders*, 4th ed., text rev. (Washington, DC: American Psychiatric Association, 2000).

describes a condition that includes antisocial or criminal behavior with special psychological and behavioral characteristics. Many mental health professionals use *psychopath/psychopathy* interchangeably with the terms *sociopath/sociopathy*. Criminologists often draw a distinction between the two terms, using sociopath/sociopathy for people who are impulsive, irresponsible, disorganized, and often violent, and reserving psychopath/ psychopathy for those whose antisocial behavior is more organized and more predatory in nature.

How Many Psychopaths Are There?

As stated previously, researchers and experts in the field believe that 1 percent of the US population meet the criteria for psychopathy. With a population of over 300 million people, that means that there may be more than 3 million true psychopaths in the United States. And, unlike people who have some other mental disorders, most psychopaths aren't loners. Many of us probably have met or will meet a psychopath or interact with one on a daily basis.

When we think of psychopaths, most of us tend to think of men. In part, this is because most of the research on psychopathy has focused on men who are in prison, not to mention that men are more likely to commit the sort of violent crimes that make headlines. But we should not ignore the substantial body of evidence from scientific research, the media, and popular culture that tells us psychopathy is a very real phenomenon among women. Research also reveals that psychopathy may look different in men than in women (see chapter 4). If current conceptions of psychopathy—based largely on research involving male subjects—do not adequately represent psychopathy as it appears in women, it may be that the diagnosis is missed in some women and their psychopathic traits are attributed to other disorders. For example, take "conning and manipulation," a standard element in the assessment of psychopathy. It has been suggested that in women, manipulation takes the form of flirtation, which is more commonly considered to be a symptom of histrionic personality disorder. Similarly, impulsivity in women may be manifested by self-harm, pointing to a diagnosis of borderline personality disorder, while in men it comes out as violence toward others and leads to a diagnosis of psychopathy or antisocial personality disorder.[23]

The History of Psychopathy

People have been doing bad things to each other since the dawn of humankind, and psychopaths are believed to exist in all cultures. Over the centuries, many different words have been used to describe individuals who appear to lack moral judgment, routinely take advantage of others, or engage in violence. According to a 1976 study by Jane M. Murphy, then an anthropologist at Harvard University, the Yupik Eskimos use the word *kunlangeta* to describe a man who continually cheats, steals, takes sexual advantage of women, and cannot be trusted to be truthful. The word *psychopathy* is derived from the Greek *psukhe* (soul) and *pathos* (disease), and means "suffering of the mind." Ironically, most psychopaths would deny that they and their minds are suffering at all. And they don't see anything wrong with their behavior.

In 1809, the French surgeon Philippe Pinel described the concept of psychopathy with the term *manie sans delire* (mania without delirium). A Scottish physician, James Prichard, used the term *moral insanity* in 1835 when describing people whose conduct consistently lacked decency and propriety, but who showed no other cognitive or behavioral abnormalities. Kurt Schneider, a German psychiatrist, used the term *psychopathic personality* in 1923 to describe "abnormal personalities" who either suffer personally because of their abnormality or make others suffer. In 1930, an American psychiatrist, George Everett Partridge, made the case that the term *sociopath* described these people more accurately, because their behavior, which was often in violation of social norms, was a societal problem. The International Classification of Diseases seems to follow this theme, as it applies a diagnosis of Dyssocial Personality to these individuals.[24]

A major advance in the twentieth-century understanding of psychopathic behavior was the work of American psychiatrist and psychoanalyst Hervey Cleckley. Cleckley worked in a psychiatric hospital in Augusta, Georgia, and in 1941 published his book *The Mask of Sanity: An Attempt to Clarify Some Issues About the So-Called Psychopathic Personality*. As the title of the book suggests, Cleckley believed that the psychopath hides his or her lack of empathy and moral constraint behind a mask of normal function and seemingly appropriate behavior.

Cleckley proposed that there were sixteen specific traits associated with psychopathy, including superficial charm and good intelligence, unreliability, untruthfulness, lack of remorse and shame, absence of delusions and anxiety, and inability to learn from experience or follow any life plan. In his book, Cleckley used a series of case examples describing people whom he characterized as psychopaths, noting their lack of conscience and empathy and hypothesizing that this resulted from an underlying psychological deficit rather than life experience. Cleckley also proposed that psychopaths are different from the rest of society by virtue of this fundamental and inherent psychological abnormality. He described them as irresponsible and impulsive, unconstrained by conscience and empathy, but not always criminal in their behavior. In fact, Cleckley was very interested in how psychopaths can survive and thrive in society.

The Hare Psychopathy Checklist

The concept of psychopathy has been with us for a very long time. Cleckley and psychoanalytic thinkers who both preceded and followed him have used the term to describe a wide range of behaviors that reflect problems people have in their interactions with the world around them. While this subjective use of the term *psychopathy* was often helpful from a clinical standpoint, the lack of consistent, valid, and reliable diagnostic criteria made it impossible to study psychopathy scientifically.

Psychopathy has received increased attention and has been the study of extensive scientific investigation over the last several decades due in large part to the groundbreaking research by psychologist Robert Hare when he was at the University of British Columbia. Hare started with the criteria developed by Cleckley and created a psychopathy checklist designed to assess both the subject's emotional state and behavioral history. This tool, known as the PCL (Psychopathy CheckList), is meant to be used by trained mental health professionals who both interview the person and review his or her personal history.[25]

Hare's checklist—now called the PCL–R, as it was revised some years ago—is the most widely used diagnostic tool in the field of psychopathy. Research has confirmed both its reliability and validity: similar results are obtained when different clinicians use the test, and the test measures an actual psychological construct or clinical entity. Over the years, the checklist has been tested extensively, and it remains the most widely accepted method of assessing psychopathy. Today, when mental health professionals and criminologists talk about psychopathy, they are most likely referencing someone who reaches the cutoff score for psychopathy on the PCL–R.

For each of the twenty items in the checklist, assessors assign a score of 0 (not present), 1 (possibly or partially present), or 2 (definitely present). The maximum possible score is 40. Assessors are typically psychologists or psychiatrists, but increasingly they may be social workers or even unlicensed individuals working in correctional settings. The scoring is meant to be dimensional. That is, it is intended to indicate the extent to which a person is similar to the "prototypical psychopath." A score in the top 25 percent of the scale (over 30) indicates that the person can be categorically designated as a psychopath. The average score for all incarcerated male offenders in the United States is in the middle range of the scale. The average person in the general population typically scores in the bottom 25 percent of the scale (10 or less).

Hare and his colleagues subsequently developed a screening version of the checklist for use in both forensic populations—those involved in the criminal justice system—and nonforensic settings. The PCL–SV (for "screening version") takes less time to administer and provides sound results when there is little or no history of criminal behavior. It considers an individual's emotions and behavior overall and in relation to others. Scoring is similar to that of the PCL–R.

Even though they are widely available in the age of the Internet, both the PCL–R and its screening version are psychological assessment instruments intended for use by trained mental health professionals who have the skill and education to use clinical judgment in evaluating responses. They should not be used by anyone without training and clinical experience, whether as a self-assessment or to assess others. In discussing psychopaths and almost psychopaths in the case studies presented in this book, we'll make reference to psychopathy as measured by the PCL–R. Such discussions will help you better understand these troubling—often destructive—almost psychopathic behaviors and provide strategies for coping with such behaviors.

Bill: A Closer Analysis

We will now consider Bill's behavior in terms of the PCL–R and the PCL–SV as we answer our original question: Why is Bill a psychopath?

One of the first things we consider is how Bill interacts with those around him: Is he straightforward and sincere, or is he superficial and charming—perhaps a bit too charming? In fact, we see that Bill has a pattern of ingratiating himself with superiors. His behavior with the psychiatrist—complimenting him, unnecessarily noting the doctor's expertise and expressing how interested he was in his opinion—are prime examples of the superficiality and glibness that often characterize psychopaths. He also engages in something we call *narcissistic twinning:* attempting to show what he has in common with the doctor as a form of persuasion and manipulation.

Bill is grandiose and thinks of himself as a very special and capable guy. For example, he was completely sincere when he told the doctor that he would have received a college scholarship had he stayed in school, and the reason he left school was that he was too advanced and was just plain bored. Even if he had some awareness that his own behavior had ended his high school career prematurely, he was unable to acknowledge that his ability or effort (or lack thereof) had anything to do with it. However, Bill's complaints about being uninterested in school, as well as his reckless driving and history of getting tired of his romantic relationships and abandoning them, indicate a tendency to be bored and a need for stimulation that are also characteristic of psychopaths.

Like other psychopaths, Bill lies—and he's pretty good at it. He falsified his military history and easily fabricated a story about the mailroom events that was completely contrary to what others observed, and he did it while on the spot and potentially in a great deal of trouble. Not only do psychopaths lie, they do it with a facility that would be almost fun to watch—if only there were no victims. Psychopaths will try to lie their way out of a situation and may keep lying even as they are backed into a corner, hoping that the questioner will eventually give up the chase. For example, we know of a case where an employee under investigation for financial misconduct in the workplace had been criminally charged with stealing a family member's credit card information. Confronted by the security officer with the charge of credit card fraud, the employee explained it away with a fascinating, indeed fantastic, tale of mistaken identity and miscommunication, ending with resolution of the charge. When the security officer asked for permission to call this particular family member—whom the

employee had actually listed as his emergency contact—
he calmly said, "Sure." The family member's response when he
was reached? "That SOB is a liar and a thief!"

The glibness and superficiality, as well as the propensity to
lie, help psychopaths succeed at yet another characteristic
behavior: manipulating and conning others. And Bill certainly
qualifies here, too, as evidenced by his behaviors with supervisors, his attempted manipulation of the examining psychiatrist,
and his ability to carry on sexual relationships with several
women at a time and get some of those women to support him
financially.

Bill's indifferent attitude about his behavior at work, his
lack of guilt for having fathered several children and avoiding
paying support, and his blaming Amy for provoking his behavior
—all point to a lack of remorse, another characteristic of psychopathy. The successful psychopath often learns to express
remorse, finding it the best way to get out of trouble, but this
contrition is invariably superficial and temporary.

Bill's inability to describe depression and his historical
incapacity to form long-term relationships are also consistent
with another characteristic of psychopathy: a limited capacity
for experiencing emotion generally and feelings of love and
attachment specifically. Some psychopaths can act as if they
have such feelings, going through the motions and mimicking
those words and behaviors that they have learned are part of a
"normal" relationship. They behave "as if" they were in love or
depressed, for example. For these people, "out of sight is out
of mind": once the person with whom they supposedly have
a relationship is out of the picture, so are any claimed feelings
of affection and attachment. For psychopaths, emotional

attachment is based on needs and social learning, not on true feeling.

One of the core characteristics of psychopathy, and one that has been studied extensively, is the lack of capacity for empathy. Empathy, the ability to recognize and appreciate the feelings of others, is generally thought to come in two forms. Cognitive empathy is the capacity to identify that another person is experiencing an emotion and to perceive what that emotion is. Emotional empathy is the capacity to actually share in the emotional experience of others. Psychopaths may lack both, and that is the case with Bill. Bill's difficulty understanding immediately how Amy may have felt in that terrifying situation, trapped in a small room with him as he raged at her and then put his fist into the wall, fully demonstrates his lack of empathy. In addition, Bill's bragging to the doctor about his skill at manipulating women and denying paternity demonstrate his obliviousness to how his behaviors and comments make others feel, not to mention his manipulation of others and indifference to his responsibilities. Psychopaths may learn enough to express something that approximates empathy, as well as remorse and other feelings, but for those like Bill, it doesn't even occur to them to fake it.

Bill's history of living off his girlfriends and his mother, his many impulsive behaviors, his involvement in many short-term relationships, his promiscuity—all point toward psychopathy, as well. To the extent that psychopaths have plans for the future, they are often unrealistic. Bill is a prime example, with his claimed intention to attend college and then law school, medical school, or perhaps both, given his history of criminal behavior and less-than-stellar academic career. Bill's impulsivity in many areas—including his outburst with Amy, throwing the handcart, and his self-description as a "free spirit" who does what he wants, when he wants—is just the sort of thing we encounter in psychopaths. The same is true for the irresponsibility Bill shows through his failure to support his children, his reckless driving, and his abandonment of relationships.

In addition to not fulfilling their responsibilities and obligations, psychopaths fail to *accept* responsibility for their own actions, as Bill does when he denies accountability for his school difficulties and behavior at work, even going so far as to blame Amy for making him angry. While not all psychopaths engage in criminal behavior, when they do, they often show versatility—getting involved in multiple types of crime. For Bill, this shows up in a history that includes an ex-fiancée's restraining order; arrests for reckless driving, for breaking and entering, and assault and battery; and further allegations of check forgery and credit card theft.

There are other characteristics of psychopaths—behavioral problems in childhood or adolescence, and failure when released on parole or probation—that we would consider in determining whether Bill meets the full criteria. But since we don't have that information, we couldn't weigh those factors if we were scoring Bill on the PCL–R. But even using only the factors that we discussed, we would find that Bill falls at the high end of the scoring, qualifying as a full-blown psychopath.

How did this story end? The psychiatrist met with the human resources director and the rest of the management team at the company and advised them of his findings. Even after hearing Bill's real history and the psychiatrist's assessment, a senior member of the team, who had always been charmed by

Bill, objected to the recommendation that Bill be terminated (even with a generous severance package). The senior member was persuaded only when the HR director threatened to quit if Bill were allowed to return to work. Such is the hold of the psychopath over some.

· · ·

At this point, you may be thinking that you've run across a psychopath or two in your lifetime, and you could well be right about that. But in the following chapters, we're going to show you that it's much more likely that you've run into someone at work, at home, or about town who is an almost psychopath, and we are going to tell you what you can do about that (or about *yourself,* if you think you're an almost psychopath).

3

The Almost Psychopath

Now that we've described the basics about true psychopaths (their intensely self-centered patterns of behavior, willingness to hurt or intimidate others to get what they want, and distinct lack of empathy and conscience) as well as how clinicians identify them (by using the PCL–R and related instruments), it is time to turn our attention to people who are almost psychopaths. As you'll see, the different factors that characterize psychopathy can come together in an almost endless number of possible combinations to describe almost psychopaths.

We begin with another life story, this one about an almost psychopath.

James

To all appearances, James was just another member of the local fire department in a small midwestern city. He and his wife, Carol—both in their late thirties—lived in the suburbs, socialized with friends, and enjoyed rock climbing and all sorts of other outdoor activities. Carol periodically raised the question of having children, but James always would suggest that they wait a few years, so they could enjoy the adventure travel they both loved before settling into parenthood.

After college, James had held a series of office jobs that never quite panned out. Each time he left a job, he would describe the problems he had with that particular position: the work was dull, the boss was stupid, he was not getting the credit he deserved, and so on. Looking for something with more excitement, he joined the fire department, where he was regarded as a decent firefighter, albeit a bit of a braggart and show-off who tended to exaggerate his "heroic" exploits and take unnecessary risks at times. A member of the search and rescue team, James often found a way to be on camera for the evening news and became resentful when he was not asked to represent the department on public occasions. James was never a big drinker or partier, and when he did socialize with people from work, it was only with the elite search and rescue team members, rather than the other firefighters, whom he regarded as more run of the mill.

James worked two twenty-four-hour shifts a week, so he had a good deal of time at home. Carol, a human resources manager for a large local company, worked five days a week, often bringing work home at night and on weekends. She initially found it sweet and romantic when James tried to get her to stay home from work to be with him. She found it less sweet and romantic, though, when he sulked at her inability to do so.

Carol knew before they got married that James had been married once before, just after he graduated from college. That marriage had ended after six months, and James explained that he and his first wife had been young and immature when they got married and both realized they had made a mistake. In light of that, Carol and James decided that living together for several years would be a good idea. In spite of his occasional bouts of somewhat childish, self-centered behavior, they got along well, did chores together at home, and enjoyed each other's company. After five years of living together, they decided to tie the knot.

Shortly after they got married, though, Carol was surprised to find that James seemed to change. Around friends, James bragged about how he had "the perfect life" and embarrassed Carol by alluding to their "amazing sex life." At home, however, he was less enamored of her. With time on his hands, he had taken up a hobby related to his lifelong enjoyment of comic books—collecting them and going to shows and conventions with other collectors. This was not an interest of Carol's, but she encouraged him because he enjoyed it. James gradually devoted more and more time to his hobby. He began going to conventions on some weekends, sometimes dressing as one of his favorite characters, even though weekends were the only time Carol had at home with him. He loved being the center of attention and often volunteered to appear at schools and children's parties as one of the cartoon characters.

Carol went along with all of this since it did not happen very often and it seemed to improve her husband's spirits. At home, she had noticed him looking increasingly sad and she felt bad that she often had some work to do on the weekends. To a certain degree, Carol was relieved that James was busy with his hobby and was no longer moping around, looking like a lonely lost puppy, even if he was spending time and money on comic books. Time and again, James explained to her that these "graphic novels," as he referred to them, were highly valuable, that he had a special ability to identify emerging talent in the field, and that he expected to be able to retire and make a fortune trading and selling these books.

Carol became annoyed when James began neglecting things around the house. Coming home from long days at the office, she would find a day's worth of dirty dishes in the sink, the laundry still not done, and the refrigerator empty—even though James had assured her that he would take care of all of those things. Instead, Carol would come home to discover that he had spent the day organizing his collection, posting to online interest groups, or some days just sleeping or watching television.

When she tried to talk with him about this, James would claim that he hadn't noticed the mess, didn't recall having been asked to do chores, or had forgotten his promise. Occasionally, he talked about feeling depressed, to which Carol responded by showing him increased attention. This always improved James's mood. Other times, he argued that he was too busy managing his "one-of-a-kind" and "extremely valuable" collection, expressing dismay that Carol didn't appreciate his unique skills. Whatever the reason for disappointing his wife, James invariably apologized and pledged to be more thoughtful. But within weeks, the old habits returned, leaving Carol with unpleasant recollections of a former relationship with a partner who had been extremely passive aggressive.

Curious about the change in James's behavior after they got married, Carol decided to do a little investigating by asking his family for details about his past. She was taken aback when they opened up about parts of his life that she had never heard—his history of being bullied and bullying others as a child, his brushes with the law as a juvenile, a history of depression in high school, and a series of troubled romantic relationships, including yet another marriage that James had never mentioned to her. Carol wondered what she had gotten herself into. Who was this person she had known and lived with for so many years?

The marriage irretrievably began to unravel one day when Carol received a letter from a woman who claimed to have been James's girlfriend for the past year, providing days, times, and places where they had been together. This woman wrote to say that she had ended her relationship with James when she learned that he had also been seeing someone else. Confronted with this, James denied spending time with this woman, or anyone else, until Carol pointed out the convincing evidence of both relationships from the letter.

Carol asked James to leave the house, and he did, but not without proclaiming his complete innocence. Although she was adamant, James begged her not to separate, as he was "clinically depressed." This surprised Carol, as she had seen none of the other signs and symptoms of depression she had learned about in her work in human resources. Carol asked James if he had seen a doctor, and James reported that he had seen his primary care physician, who had given him a clean bill of health. James also said that he was seeing a psychiatrist for medication and was engaged in therapy; he said he had not told Carol about this before because he did not want to worry her. When Carol asked to speak with the therapist and psychiatrist and offered to go to sessions with him, James appeared anxious and turned her down.

Suspicious, Carol looked into their health insurance utilization (they were insured through her employer) and found that James had no mental health charges at all—no therapy and no medication—although James had, in fact, seen his primary care doctor. James became angry upon learning of Carol's investigation of this—outraged that Carol did not believe him—and blamed his depression and their marital problems on Carol being controlling, self-centered, and neglectful of him.

Finally, Carol had had enough. She insisted that James move out, and she then began divorce proceedings. James continued to come back to the house while Carol was at work, leaving her gifts as well as love notes. One day, Carol discovered that pieces of jewelry she had inherited from her grandmother and some other valuable heirlooms were missing. She contacted the police, who found no evidence of a break-in. They interviewed James (who denied taking anything), told him to stay out of the house, and advised Carol to change the locks. After that, she received hang-up phone calls for a while and also had the distinct sense that someone was walking around outside the house on some nights. Convinced that she was just being paranoid, she dismissed her concerns, but just in case, she told her divorce attorney about the incidents. After some communication between her attorney and James's and some increased police presence in the neighborhood, things quieted down.

What Makes an "Almost Psychopath"?

Why do we say that James is an almost psychopath and not a true psychopath, like Bill from the last chapter? Both men seem to have difficulty pursuing long-range goals, appear to be pretty comfortable with deception, and are far more focused on themselves than anyone else in their lives. Are they the same or are they fundamentally different? And how? The answer to both questions lies in both the quantity and quality of the psychopathic traits Bill and James possess and exhibit. And that somewhat ambiguous answer is the key to understanding what we mean by being an almost psychopath.

The Difference Is One of Degree

It's critical to recognize that the distinction between a psychopath and an almost psychopath is based not on the types of behaviors and emotional limitations but rather on the frequency and intensity of the behaviors and emotional (or, more accurately, emotionless) reactions to others. Almost psychopaths, like true psychopaths, may engage in socially unacceptable and sometimes illegal conduct, and again like true psychopaths, they may be self-centered, egotistical, and indifferent to the needs and emotions of others. *The only real difference is the degree to which they exhibit these traits compared with true psychopaths.*

By definition, almost psychopaths share some of the characteristics of true psychopaths. Almost psychopaths, like James, can be narcissistic and grandiose, seeing themselves as superior to other people and not bound by society's rules and customs. They can be manipulative, comfortable with lying, and quite capable of justifying their actions, often by blaming others for their behavior, such as Bill's statement that "She shouldn't have pissed me off."

On the other hand, almost psychopaths may worry about getting caught and find themselves weaving an increasingly elaborate web of lies to make themselves look better and to cover their past lies and deceptions. While they may well establish relationships, almost psychopaths will often have charm and glibness, as well as relatively shallow emotions that are much more intellectual than emotional. They can talk about emotions, but their descriptions lack any real sense of the feelings that accompany the emotions. Even when their lies are discovered, any words of remorse are just that—words. Because they want to live by their own rules and are typically impulsive and irresponsible, almost psychopaths may be unable to reach long-term goals or maintain meaningful long-term relationships. They may engage in aggressive and inappropriate conduct, ranging from harassment and stalking behaviors to thefts and malicious gossip.

Again, a good way to think of it is that the distinction between almost psychopaths and true psychopaths is based on the intensity or frequency of the inappropriate behavior and emotional dysfunction. Someone whose life has been thoroughly dominated by illegal or socially inappropriate behaviors and callous, emotionally barren relationships (frequently in prison for violent crimes, has a string of failed marriages and estranged children) is probably a true psychopath. Someone who shows a lower level of inappropriate conduct and troubled relationships (gets in hot water on the job for occasionally using company tools and stolen materials to do side jobs, serially cheats on a spouse or girlfriend/boyfriend) is more likely an almost psychopath.

Unlike their psychopath counterparts, people who are almost psychopaths are capable of living more easily among the general population and maintaining relationships, with less frequent harm to those with whom they are involved. The almost psychopath is not likely to be the ideal employee, neighbor, spouse, or parent but may be able to get along well enough to keep steady employment (although perhaps at a series of jobs) and maintain relationships (probably ones that others might describe as toxic). The almost psychopath uses others for personal gain but is careful not to irretrievably push those people away. And if he or she does overstep, the almost psychopath effortlessly generates a string of excuses, apologies, and promises in an effort to preserve the relationship and future opportunities for personal satisfaction. This ability to function well enough to maintain a place in society (as opposed to prison or a treatment facility) is one of the major reasons that you are likely to run into almost psychopaths in the first place.

It's Also a Difference of Degree between Almost Psychopathic and Normal Behavior

Virtually everyone engages in improper behavior once in a while. Remember our colleague who begins his talks by asking who in the audience has ever told even the smallest lie or taken a pen from work? Technically, he is suggesting that we are all liars and thieves. Who hasn't violated the speed limit or jay-walked or otherwise displayed their own "superego lacunae"? And at times, most of us have a somewhat inflated view of our abilities and accomplishments, engage in manipulative behavior (ever exaggerate the sniffles a bit to get some extra attention from a loved one?), and now and again seemingly "turn off" our conscience so we don't feel bad about taking advantage of someone else's misfortune. Does that make everyone an almost psychopath? Absolutely not.

As with the difference between psychopaths and almost psychopaths, the key to determining the difference between almost psychopaths and the rest of us is the frequency and intensity of the aberrant conduct and the emotional response to that behavior. Is one really atrocious act enough? How about two? And just how bad or strange does the behavior or the interaction have to be? (This is where it's so important to seek the judgment and expertise of clinicians before we start attaching labels to people.)

If last week you took credit for a co-worker's success and in retrospect you feel guilty about it, you are probably not an almost psychopath. That is an isolated incident, and besides, emotional discomfort is not something an almost psychopath would feel; instead, an almost psychopath would likely feel deserving of the unwarranted praise and would see the hapless co-worker whose thunder he or she stole as a weak person who isn't worthy of the credit anyway. Whereas the rest of us might well fess up, or at least go out of our way to make amends with our co-worker, the almost psychopath—like the real thing—likely has little to no conscience to soothe. He or she may lie low for a while, but when another opportunity arises to do the same thing, this person will find it hard to resist.

It's when a person has a *history* and pattern of self-serving and uncaring behavior that he or she moves from the realm of someone with "normal" behavior, which includes the occasional acceptable (if not encouraged) "bad" acts, to become an almost psychopath. There is no precise point at which this happens, but if a person's life and character is defined by a series of self-serving decisions reflecting an uncaring attitude toward others, the person is likely an almost psychopath. This distinction is reflected in the way the PCL–R is used to identify almost psychopaths and true psychopaths. The professionals who use the assessment assume that no one will score a zero— no one lives the perfectly altruistic life, sacrificing the self entirely to the needs of others. Instead, a reasonable point is chosen at which immoral and dishonest behavior coupled with a lack of remorse shows that a person is different enough from most people to be called an almost psychopath.

One more thing. Perhaps at some point the idea has flickered through your mind that you might be a true psychopath (or an almost psychopath). Maybe it was after clearly crossing some legal or social boundary, or even after someone said the word to you. (People like to throw the word *psychopath* around even if they don't know what it really means.) In fact, reading this book might give you pause.

If you are concerned because you have had some troubling thoughts, remember what we pointed out earlier: normal people can have dark fantasies and even do some wrong things, but that does not put them on the psychopath spectrum. As you analyze your private self, though, keep this in mind: if the idea that you are or could be a psychopath makes you feel anxious, if you find those dark thoughts repugnant, then you probably *aren't* at high risk. A true psychopath, or even an almost psychopath, wouldn't give it more than a passing thought. So, somewhat counterintuitively, if you are worried about being a psychopath of any kind, you are probably at fairly low risk—although you certainly should consider addressing some of the behaviors and feelings that are triggering the concern. On the other hand, if you have considered the possibility that you may be a psychopath and haven't felt particularly anxious or distressed by that, or maybe took a certain pride in it, there may be a real problem. In either case, your awareness that something is amiss in your behavior or feelings means that you have gotten a sense of your own dark side. That awareness is the first step in understanding and perhaps changing those behaviors and developing a greater capacity to relate to others. As we will discuss in later chapters, help is available if you want it.

Antisocial Behavior: A Continuum

When considering people who engage in behaviors that offend, distress, or harm others, we have learned through time and experience that it is often less helpful to think in terms of formal and official diagnostic criteria for psychopathy or the personality disorders that clearly define these conditions. Most people don't neatly fit into the classic, formal diagnostic criteria. People are complicated, and their behavior tends to vary widely, even when they share certain diagnostic traits. In talking about the almost psychopath concept, we find it useful to focus instead on these ten key indicators that seem to capture the characteristics of the almost psychopaths you are most likely to encounter. This list does not include the more obvious socially deviant traits of psychopathic behavior, as identified in the PCL–R. To decide if this is someone you know or care about—or perhaps you yourself—answer the questions on the "Ten Key Indicators" list that follows.

If you reflect for a moment on these questions, you can probably see how they relate to the diagnostic criteria we used in our analysis of Bill. They are, in a word, on the same *spectrum*, only a bit less severe than true psychopathy. If yes answers apply when you run through all these questions, the person you are considering (including yourself) has probably not yet committed a major crime or ended up in jail but may be at risk for damaging his or her life or the lives of others. And if you answer yes to even some of these questions, it is probably time

to start thinking about whether, and how, certain behav.
can be changed.

Looking around, it seems obvious that, as with most things, the world is not sharply divided into two groups of people—good and evil. Rather, it consists of a wide range of people and

Almost Psychopaths: Ten Key Indicators

1. Are they superficially charming and glib, with an answer for everything?

2. Is there a lack of empathy, i.e., an impaired ability to understand and appreciate the emotions of others and the impact of their behavior on other people?

3. Confronted with a difficult moral choice, do they more often than not rationalize and arrive at a decision to act in their own self-interest?

4. Do they lie repeatedly, including when it is unnecessary or for minor reasons?

5. Are they conning and manipulative?

6. When they get criticized for something, is it always some-one else's fault?

7. When they cause harm or hurt to others, is there a lack of true remorse?

8. Do they seem to have limited capacity to experience and express feelings for others or maintain relationships?

9. Do they find it easy to ignore responsibilities?

10. Do people and situations exist solely for the purpose of gratifying their needs and wants?

behaviors, the majority of whom do not dwell permanently on one or the other side of the good-evil divide. From our perspective, the world looks something like this:

Almost Psychopathy Scale

Socially Acceptable Common Behaviors and Thoughts	The Almost Psychopath	Condition Meets Diagnostic Criteria for Full-Blown Psychopathy

Subclinical Psychopathy

We have been using the term *almost psychopaths* to describe people like James who demonstrate some of the behavioral and emotional aberrations of true psychopaths but to a lesser degree. Just as the psychopathy checklists assess ranges of emotions and behaviors, we are considering the almost psychopath as lying somewhere along a continuum. As we mentioned in chapter 1, another term is used in the medical community for such a person—*subclinical psychopath*. This term, as well as *subsyndromal psychopath*, is generally accepted by psychiatrists, psychologists, and researchers.

The words *subclinical* and *subsyndromal* are used in medicine —not just psychiatry—to describe any abnormal condition where the symptoms do not rise to the level that meets the diagnostic criteria for the disease. For example, there is subclinical hyperthyroidism when the abnormal thyroid activity is minimal or in its early stage, and subclinical depression when an individual has some low-level symptoms of depression but does not meet the diagnostic criteria. In both cases, the person is only mildly affected and may not even be aware a problem exists. The basic idea behind the general terms *subclinical* and *subsyndromal* is that the medical community realizes that, in some circumstances, a person could have a measurable and identifiable problem even before that person's condition reaches an agreed-upon standard of significance and meets the criteria for the diagnosis.

Naturally, subclinical psychopathy presents fewer behaviors or traits than those identified in the technical categorical definition of psychopathy—which generally means a person scores below the top 25 percent maximum score on the PCL–R (or its screening version) but higher than the bottom 25 percent on the scale.

Every person would likely score *something* on either version of the checklist. The subclinical definitions need to have a floor, or everyone would be considered a subclinical psychopath. And that is the way we define the subclinical or almost psychopath in this book. So as we move forward, keep in mind that our definition of an almost psychopath is a person who would score in the broad middle range on the PCL–R or PCL–SV checklist. In many ways, the idea of the almost psychopath captures the older definitions of psychopathy in which different types of psychopathic traits were used to identify subcategories of psychopaths.

You might think that this definition of subclinical psychopathy as a numeric score is somewhat arbitrary; after all, what's the real difference between scores that are above the average range but only a point or two apart? Probably not much. And perhaps there is a gray area where it is a toss-up whether to include or exclude the person as a subclinical psychopath. Both checklists are tools that can measure the entire range: from a (hypothetical) person who is perfectly selfless and caring and scores a 0, to the serial murderer who tops out at the maximum score. (We can't think of anyone who would get a 0, but think Ted Bundy at the high end.) *Where* we draw the lines is a func-

An Evolutionary Strategy?

Some researchers believe that psychopathy itself is actually a survival strategy that helps humans continue on in times of threat to the individual or his or her group. It is considered pathological only when it is out of place and harms others in the social group. In fact, there is evidence that some traits seen in psychopathy can be helpful to achieving high levels of function-ing and psychological health. In his seminal works on psycho-paths, Cleckley described psychopaths as charming, possessing above-average intelligence, lacking in delusions and neurotic behaviors, and having a reduced risk of completed suicide. (Why kill yourself if you don't see anything wrong with how you are?) Overall, these are positive traits. Studies have shown that certain aspects of psychopathy are *negatively* related to stress and *positively* related to measures of verbal intelligence and socio-economic status. Subclinical psychopathy has been associated with heightened self-esteem and positive first impressions. No problems in any of that, so long as those strengths are used for good rather than evil (or at least are not used to intentionally manipulate and take advantage of others).

We are not suggesting that being an almost psychopath or a true psychopath is a good thing. Nevertheless, understanding that despite the harm they inflict, true psychopaths and, per-haps even more commonly, almost psychopaths have certain "strengths" that allow them to fit in, beguile, and manipulate us is an important step in recognizing them for who they really are.

tion of experience and judgment. Yes, a person scoring significantly higher than average on the PCL–R could be considered a true psychopath, but most who work and conduct research in this field agree that a score at the threshold of the top 25 percent on the scale is the appropriate point where a person in the forensic setting displays enough signs and symptoms to warrant the diagnosis of psychopath. Even so, there is a point where it makes sense to consider a person dysfunctional enough to be called a subclinical psychopath as opposed to someone who occasionally manipulates her co-workers or lies to her boss and is simply considered an annoying person who is best avoided whenever possible. And as we have pointed out elsewhere, our goal is not to encourage you to label people but instead to help you gain a better understanding of people's behavior.

How Many Almost Psychopaths Are There?

It's impossible to know the exact number of subclinical psychopaths in the United States or any country, for that matter. And as we will point out, behaviors that hint at psychopathy, as problematic as they may be, do not necessarily indicate that a person is a true psychopath or an almost psychopath. While true psychopaths are often recognized after encounters with the criminal justice system, almost psychopaths are much less likely to commit crimes that would result in incarceration or court-ordered psychological or psychiatric treatment. Nevertheless, some research indicates that there are far more almost psychopaths than true psychopaths in the general population. Studies that examined the prevalence of subclinical psychopathy in student populations in the United States and Sweden showed rates in the range of 5 to 15 percent.[26] (The studies used the same questionnaire, and the rate was actually somewhat higher in Sweden than in the United States.)

Since most experts believe that only 1 percent of the general US population qualify as psychopaths, the odds are far greater

---

Why Didn't I See It?

A common question people ask themselves after dealing with an almost psychopath is: *How did I not see this while it was happening?* Part of the answer is surely that the almost psychopath did what psychopaths do—charm and manipulate, con and lie. But part of the answer probably lies within you as well. You didn't "see" it because, literally, you can't think the way a psychopath does.

> William March, author of *The Bad Seed*, put it well:
>
> [G]ood people are rarely suspicious; they cannot imagine others doing the things they themselves are incapable of doing; usually they accept the undramatic solution as the correct one, and let matters rest there. Then too, the normal are inclined to visualize the [psychopath] as one who's as monstrous in appearance as he is in mind, which is about as far from the truth as one could well get. . . . These monsters of real life usually looked and behaved in a more normal manner than their actually normal brothers and sisters; they presented a more convincing picture of virtue than virtue presented of itself—just as the wax rosebud or the plastic peach seemed more perfect to the eye, more what the mind thought a rosebud or peach should be, than the imperfect original from which it had been modeled.[27]

If you've been used and fooled by an almost psychopath, don't be embarrassed—accept it as part of the price of having empathy and an inclination to see the good in people. But that doesn't mean you have to let it happen again.

---

that you will run into, work for, date, marry, raise, or live next door to an almost psychopath than a true psychopath. Additionally, your chances of coming into contact with an almost psychopath are a lot better than, say, your odds of winning the lottery; 5 to 15 percent of the population means that for every twenty people, up to three of them may fall within the almost psychopath range.

While these almost psychopaths will exhibit different disruptive behaviors with varying degrees of intensity over time, *all* of these people may engage in some combination of destructive, unethical conduct and display the self-centered personality that are hallmarks of the almost psychopath. With the probabilities being what they are, it is highly likely that you have or have had an almost psychopath in your life or that you may identify some of these traits in yourself.

James: A Closer Look

Is James an almost psychopath? In fact, he exhibits and possesses a number of the traits that we find in psychopaths: grandiosity, manipulation of others, lying, not fulfilling his responsibilities, having unrealistic goals for the future, and not taking responsibility for his own behavior, as well as some degree of superficiality, impulsivity, and need for stimulation. Those are all serious, and they do earn James a spot along the psychopathy continuum, but he would not rank as a full-blown psychopath.

Setting aside the question of how James might have scored on the two formal diagnostic instruments, let's think about James in terms of who he is as a person. What would it be like to deal with James in the workplace? As a friend or as a romantic partner? We've tried to capture that experience in this case example, but you may be able to paint a more complete picture when you think about people you know who exhibit some of the same characteristics—and even yourself. As we go through the next chapters and their case examples, you may well find that the almost psychopaths we describe are a part of your life or the lives of people you care about, and you may feel encouraged to do something about it.

4

Could It Be Something Else?

Some years ago, a fifty-year-old professor of medicine at a New England university noticed that his previously docile and neutered cat was suddenly bringing large numbers of injured or dead birds and mice onto his front lawn. Both the professor and his housemate were surprised to see the cat, which had never shown any prowess as a hunter, attacking victims with previously unseen gusto. The professor concluded, "My cat has become a murderer!"

Curiously, at about this same time, the professor's housemate noticed a disturbing change in *the professor*. The professor himself became much more aggressive toward the housemate than he had ever been before. The housemate reported that the professor was easily provoked, had begun using harsh language and a menacing voice when he didn't get his way, and even displayed a new violent streak—kicking his "misbehaving" cat on more than one occasion. Understandably concerned about the uncharacteristic belligerence and the possibility of being likewise assaulted, the housemate moved out.

What was going on?

Were both cat and owner, by coincidence, having a really bad week and venting through aggressive outbursts? Had some calamitous event traumatized both enough to change their basic personalities? More ominously still, had they simultaneously and spontaneously become psychopaths or almost psychopaths (or the feline equivalent), or revealed previously concealed traits?

None of the above.

It turned out that this was all caused by a tick or, to be more precise, a fear of ticks, which led the professor to begin applying a commercially available tick powder on his cat. Even though the professor was cautious and wore gloves and a surgical mask while applying the treatment, a cloud of the powder would sometimes blow over him, and in the course of each day he frequently handled and petted the cat. Over the ten days or so after he began liberally applying the treatment, the professor had noted some unusual symptoms in himself, like fatigue, joint pain, and swollen eyes, but until his housemate moved out, he was unaware of the extreme change in his own personality.

Upon reflection, the professor and the temporarily displaced housemate came to suspect these symptoms were related to the tick powder; within a week of the professor discontinuing use of the powder, his cat stopped hunting and the housemate moved back in. The professor and his cat had both been affected by an ingredient in the powder (a cholinesterase inhibitor), which research has since linked to worsening temper, irritability, paranoia, and increased aggression.

Shared Symptoms

The "cat and the professor" story, while true (the case study was published in 1986[28]), is highly unusual. Nonetheless, it does illustrate an important point: things aren't always what they seem. Someone who met the professor for the first time shortly after he began exhibiting the disturbingly volatile demeanor, perhaps observing the professor kick his cat or behave aggressively to others, might have thought, "This guy is a psychopath!"

Of course, we can't conclude that a person is a psychopath or an almost psychopath without having information about his or her patterns of behavior and emotions over time. You should also understand that some antisocial behaviors and emotional deficits characteristic of psychopathy and almost psychopathy can be related to other problems—everything from chemical exposures to underlying medical conditions to other psychiatric diagnoses. If you are dealing with someone who appears to lack empathy and is so self-serving that he or she will break any rule to attain a desired outcome, you may well have an almost psychopath (or true psychopath) in your life. But it's important to remember that the complex and wide-ranging set of emotional deficits and behaviors characteristic of almost psychopathy and true psychopathy can and do overlap with other medical and psychological diagnoses.

In fact, experts in psychopathy sometimes distinguish *primary* from *secondary* psychopathy.[29] With primary psychopathy, the characteristic behaviors and emotional experiences of psychopathy are the result of something fundamentally and inherently different about the person that prevents him or her from experiencing the world as others do or controlling his or her behavior. In secondary psychopathy, those same symptoms are the product of some other deficit or abnormality that may be innate or acquired, such as low intelligence, increased sex drive, high anxiety, a tendency toward distorted or psychotic thinking, or any other condition that makes the person vulnerable to engaging in antisocial behavior.

So when you think you might be dealing with an almost psychopath, it is important to at least consider that something else may explain the person's antisocial conduct and self-interested attitude. It is *possible* that the same antisocial behavior can be the product of a fundamental lack of empathy (primary psychopathy) or arise from a number of other possible conditions, both psychological and physiological. How do we sort those out and decide which it is?

Doctors do this sort of thing all the time; it's called making a *differential diagnosis*. To arrive at a differential diagnosis, a given condition, usually called the presenting problem or chief complaint, is examined through a process of elimination—all health considerations that could possibly explain the presenting problem are considered. The idea is to correctly identify the condition, its causes, and the best possible treatment. The differential diagnosis itself is the list of conditions that might account for the symptoms in question, ranked from most to least probable. Doctors are trained to start with the most common diagnosis: medical students are taught the adage "When you hear hoofbeats, think horses, not zebras." Only when the simpler diagnosis has been ruled out is it appropriate to move on to more exotic conditions.

Even if you are not a doctor, you can begin to think about your situation as a doctor would. The usefulness of this approach is this: before you can figure out how to deal with a person who is causing pain in your life (or the pain you are causing others), you need to uncover the root of the pain, what it is that is causing this person (or you) to behave and feel that way. Once you've learned what the underlying problem is, you can better decide what to do based on the specific situation. Devising a plan to manage your relationship with a person who has bipolar disorder, for example, will be considerably different from figuring out what to do when your boss or spouse is an almost psychopath.

The following are some, but not all, of the conditions and circumstances that may also produce the same behaviors and emotional experiences common with almost psychopathy. All of these potential diagnoses are discussed in the APA's diagnostic manual, which is meant to cover any condition that could affect a person's mental health. (For more information on the current edition of this manual, known as the *DSM–IV–TR*, see appendix B.) Some of the conditions relevant to the differential diagnosis of almost psychopathy can be treated through medication, therapy, or a combination of the two and the symptoms (antisocial behavior) can be minimized. Others are currently not receptive to therapeutic management.

Let's start with some of the conditions that are treatable, if not curable.

Medical Conditions

The first item to be considered in any differential diagnosis of a mental disorder is an underlying medical illness. A wide variety of medical and surgical conditions, as well as medications, can cause changes in emotions and behavior. Brain tumors, infections, liver and kidney disease, cardiac conditions, and endocrine disorders such as thyroid disease and diabetes can all produce symptoms of mental disorders, including depression, mania, psychosis, anxiety disorders, dementia, and even changes in personality.

Bipolar Disorder

People with bipolar disorder tend to alternate between a depressed mood and a mood that is either irritable or very good—often too good. These "swings" from depression to mania can be very quick, and a subcategory of bipolar disorder is referred to as rapid cycling. Bipolar disorder was previously called manic depression. The textbook case was thought to require two distinct phases—a manic phase and a depressed phase—although we now recognize that "mixed state" bipolar disorder, in which a person simultaneously experiences both manic and depressive symptoms, is very common. Bipolar disorder is divided into type I and type II. In type I, the person has experienced at least one full-blown manic episode as well as depressive episodes. In type II, the person may never be manic, as defined below, but has hypomanic symptoms—essentially less intense manic symptoms without the psychosis. A third category, bipolar III, has been suggested to include individuals with depression who become hypomanic as a result of taking antidepressant medication.

The manic or other phase can last from days to months and can include the following symptoms:

1. Poor temper control
2. Reckless behavior and lack of self-control
3. Distractability
4. Poor judgment
5. Promiscuity

6. Spending sprees

7. Impulsive travel

8. Very elevated mood

9. Hyperactivity

10. Increased energy

11. Psychosis

Some of these symptoms (recklessness, promiscuity, poor temper control) are also part of the antisocial behavior patterns of an almost psychopath and other personality disorders, while other symptoms (hyperactivity, very elevated mood, increased energy) might lead a person with bipolar disorder to come up with the same type of grandiose and unrealistic plans as an almost psychopath. There is a high rate of comorbidity, or coexistence, of substance abuse and bipolar disorder. For some people with bipolar disorder, abusing substances is a means of self-medication, and for others it is part of the impulsive and self-destructive behavior associated with the condition.

Nevertheless, unlike an almost psychopath, in most cases a person with bipolar disorder will eventually enter a depressed phase, demonstrating symptoms that may include these:

1. Daily low mood

2. Difficulty concentrating

3. Fatigue

4. Feelings of guilt and worthlessness

5. Loss of self-esteem

6. Thoughts of suicide and death

These are not the emotions of a psychopath or of most almost psychopaths. An almost psychopath is very unlikely to feel guilt over anything and even less likely to feel genuinely suicidal. (Why would you want to kill yourself if you are better than everyone else?) However, both true psychopaths and almost psychopaths may use threats of suicide to manipulate others. Almost psychopaths are also unlikely to have prolonged periods of daily sadness; they may be frustrated or unhappy when they don't get what they want, but that is much more likely to spawn daily periods of plotting and antisocial conduct than it is feelings of joylessness. James, as you may recall, appeared depressed and lonely when he was not getting the attention he wanted from Carol.

Sleep disturbance can occur in both mania and depression, and people who are depressed can become very agitated—referred to as *psychomotor agitation*—making the diagnostic distinction somewhat difficult at times. In fact, sleep deprivation can be a major trigger for the onset of a manic episode as well as depression.

Major Depression

For someone to be diagnosed with a major depressive episode, or one of the related disorders involving major depression, the person must have at least of five of the nine symptoms listed in the *DSM–IV–TR* for at least two weeks, one of which must be either depressed mood or loss of enjoyment in activities that were previously pleasurable.[30] Some other symptoms include:

1. Significant weight loss or gain (more than 5 percent of body weight), or increase or decrease in appetite

2. Fatigue or loss of energy

3. Feelings of worthlessness or inappropriate guilt

4. Indecisiveness or diminished concentration

5. Recurrent thoughts of death or suicide

The technical term for diminished interest or pleasure is *anhedonia*—a Greek word meaning "lack of pleasure." The *DSM–IV–TR* lists formal criteria for major depressive episodes, which many clinicians remember by using a mnemonic device crafted by one of Ron's former colleagues at Massachusetts General Hospital, Dr. Carey Gross. The mnemonic is SIG E CAPS: a takeoff on the way prescriptions used to be written in Latin, and roughly translating as "Take (SIG) Energy (E) Capsules (CAPS)."

The S in SIG E CAPS stands for sleep disturbance, the I for loss of interest or anhedonia. G stands for elevated levels of guilt, as well as low self-esteem and feelings of hopelessness and helplessness. E represents low energy or fatigue, C is for decreased concentration, and A is for decreased or increased appetite. P stands for psychomotor retardation or agitation— something that is more generally observed than reported by the patient. And finally, S stands for suicidal ideation—thoughts related to suicide that range from "I wouldn't care if I died in my sleep" and "Life isn't worth living" to active plans for suicide.

Narcissistic Personality Disorder

Narcissistic personality disorder is a pervasive pattern of grandiosity, need for admiration, and lack of empathy, as indicated by five or more of the following:

1. Has a grandiose sense of self-importance, demonstrated by exaggerating achievements and talents

2. Is preoccupied by fantasies of unlimited success, brilliance, power, beauty, or ideal love

3. Believes that he or she is "special" and should only associate with other special, high-status people or institutions

4. Requires excessive admiration

5. Has a sense of entitlement, with unrealistic expectations of especially favorable treatment or automatic compliance with his or her expectations

6. Is interpersonally exploitative; takes advantage of others to achieve his or her own ends

7. Lacks empathy; is unwilling to recognize or identify with the feelings and needs of others

8. Is often envious of others

9. Displays an arrogant, haughty attitude[31]

Although lack of empathy and taking advantage of others are *part* of the diagnosis (as with almost psychopaths), people with narcissistic personality disorder (narcissists) generally don't show a history of serious antisocial behavior; their sense of entitlement might spur them to ignore social conventions or even become involved in behavior that isn't strictly legal, but they are less likely to engage in systematic rule breaking the way many almost psychopaths do.

Narcissists are obsessively concerned with how others view them; they want to be held in high esteem by everyone and employ a variety of strategies to accomplish that specific goal. Almost psychopaths share this sense of entitlement and the need to be admired, as well as the tendency to become angry and frustrated when that need is not met. Almost psychopaths (and true psychopaths), however, may be more inclined to act out maliciously when frustrated that their needs are not being met or when disappointed that they are not receiving all they feel entitled to. Narcissistic personality disorder, like antisocial personality disorder, is more commonly diagnosed in men than women.

Borderline Personality Disorder and Histrionic Personality Disorder

Listed in the same *DSM–IV–TR* diagnostic group as narcissistic personality disorder, these two diagnoses are made primarily, but not exclusively, in women. Borderline personality disorder and histrionic personality disorder are difficut conditions, and some of the behaviors and emotions associated with them may suggest that the person falls into the almost psychopath range. As mentioned earlier, some researchers have suggested that the symptoms of both these disorders may actually be the female version of some psychopathic symptoms that men experience. In other words, people with these disorders may not just resemble psychopaths or almost psychopaths; they may actually be psychopaths or almost psychopaths. Let's look at the symptoms of borderline personality disorder and histrionic personality disorder, both as individual diagnoses and as possible evidence for psychopathy itself.

The symptoms of borderline personality disorder include:

1. Frantic efforts to avoid real or imagined abandonment
2. A pattern of unstable and intense interpersonal relationships characterized by alternating between extremes of idealization and devaluation
3. Identity disturbance: markedly and persistently unstable self-image or sense of self

4. Impulsivity in at least two areas that are potentially self-damaging (e.g., promiscuous sex, eating disorders, binge eating, substance abuse, reckless driving)

5. Recurrent suicidal behavior, gestures, threats, or self-injuring behavior such as cutting, interfering with the healing of scars (excoriation), or picking at oneself

6. Affective instability due to a marked reactivity of mood (e.g., intense episodic dysphoria, irritability, or anxiety, usually lasting a few hours and only rarely more than a few days)

7. Chronic feelings of emptiness

8. Inappropriate anger or difficulty controlling anger (e.g., frequent displays of temper, constant anger, recurrent physical fights)

9. Transient, stress-related paranoid ideation, delusions, or severe dissociative symptoms[32]

Other than the symptoms related to impulsivity and anger, a reading of the *DSM–IV–TR* symptoms of borderline personality disorder does not conjure up the image of psychopaths we've presented so far. But extreme forms of borderline personality disorder can resemble psychopathy more than this list suggests and definitely raises the question of almost psychopathy. The origins of the term *borderline* indicate just how serious this condition can be. When the concept was first developed, "borderline" was used to designate that people with this condition are on the *border* between neurosis (run-of-the-mill psychological concerns experienced by many relatively high-functioning people) and psychosis.

The efforts of people with borderline personality disorder to avoid real or imagined abandonment can include threats, lying, and manipulation of such a degree that they have a real "psychopath feel" to them. And the tendency to alternately idealize and then devalue the people with whom they have relationships can similarly feel extremely manipulative and self-serving. In this regard, people with this disorder often engage in something called *splitting:* behaving in such a way that they pit people in their lives against each other in an effort to meet their own needs. A major difference between people with borderline personality disorder and those who are almost or full-blown psychopaths relates to their emotional experience. In borderline personality disorder, rather than being unable to experience emotion, the emotional experience is intense and overwhelming for the person, often leading to self-harm, such as cutting or burning, or suicide attempts.

So borderline personality disorder may look like almost psychopathy, and some of the symptoms may be shared. But is it possible that women who are psychopaths or almost psychopaths are being misdiagnosed as borderline? We think it is, although there is insufficient research at this point to prove it. Here's the argument: First, as others have suggested, psychopathic traits may be expressed differently in women than in men. In other words, female psychopaths may look different from male psychopaths, at least in some ways. Second, some of the diagnostic criteria for borderline personality disorder as they stand now may be appropriate to consider as evidence of psychopathy, but due to a cultural bias against diagnosing psychopathy in women, they are instead attributed to borderline personality disorder.

What about histrionic personality disorder? People with this disorder are less likely than those with borderline personality disorder to make us think of full-blown psychopaths. Yet, as with borderline personality disorder, we have to consider that some of its symptoms may actually suggest that someone belongs in the almost psychopath category or may represent symptoms of a slightly different presentation of psychopathy. Take a look at the diagnostic criteria for histrionic personality disorder:

1. Uncomfortable in situations in which he or she is not the center of attention

2. Interaction with others is often characterized by inappropriate sexually seductive or provocative behavior

3. Displays rapidly shifting and shallow expressions of emotions

4. Consistently uses physical appearance to draw attention to self

5. Has a style of speech that is excessively impressionistic and lacking in detail

6. Shows self-dramatization, theatricality, and exaggerated expression of emotion

7. Is suggestible, i.e., easily influenced by others or circumstances

8. Considers relationships to be more intimate than they actually are[33]

Of these criteria, several might be reminiscent or indicative of psychopathic traits. Acting or looking overly seductive (flirting) may well represent manipulative behavior or actual

Christiana: A "Mean Girl" Grows Up

If women can be psychopaths, then they can certainly be almost psychopaths. Consider this: Growing up, did you know any girls who might be considered bullies, girls who made your life miserable in school and who seemed to lack empathy? The idea of "mean girls" has caught on in popular culture, perhaps because, sadly, it strikes a chord for many of us. The *New York Times* bestseller *Queen Bees and Wannabees* by Rosalind Wiseman and the American teen comedy-drama inspired by it, *Mean Girls*, reflect a fascination with how high school social cliques operate and affect teenage girls. Certainly the subject resonates with many people, and perhaps part of the reason is that most of us know female almost psychopaths.

What might one of these mean girls look like as an adult? For an example, take the case of Christiana. Her mood swings, angry outbursts, constant lying, and manipulation of classmates, co-workers, family members, and friends—as long as they lasted as friends—would easily earn her a diagnosis of borderline personality disorder. As an adolescent, Christiana was one of the "cool kids." She bullied classmates and ran with a clique that was straight out of a *Mean Girls* script. Beginning in high school, she had multiple failed relationships and an employment history marked by firings for insubordination or her quitting because her co-workers and bosses were "stupid."

Christiana was unmarried and twenty-one when she gave birth to her daughter, Angelica, and she soon found that being a mother cramped her lifestyle. The child's father lived with her for a time, but she ultimately threw him out when she discovered that he had slept with another woman—even though Christiana herself was involved with another man.

CONTINUED ON NEXT PAGE

CONTINUED FROM PREVIOUS PAGE

Christiana's sister and parents adored Angelica, and Christiana took full advantage of their attachment to the girl. Christiana often dropped Angelica off at her parents' or sister's house and asked them to mind the child for a few hours. She would then stay out drinking with her friends until early in the morning. When she returned, she would lie, saying her car had broken down or she had fallen asleep or a friend needed help. She might even claim that she had told them she would be staying out so late. When confronted about these lies, Christiana would fly into a rage, verbally (and on a few occasions, physically) assaulting her family. Several times she decided to punish her parents and sister by refusing to let them see Angelica, telling them they would never see the child again if they didn't apologize for their alleged wrong. These relatives always gave in to Christiana's demands, partly to calm her down, but mostly because they recognized that Angelica's visits with them were the most normal, stable days of the child's life. Despite all this support, Christiana frequently told acquaintances stories about her "abusive" parents and "mean" sister.

Statistically, the overwhelming majority of people diagnosed with psychopathy are men, and the opposite is true for borderline personality disorder—most are women. Therefore, it's not surprising that most mental health professionals reviewing this case would likely conclude that Christiana has borderline personality disorder. In some ways, she is a classic borderline. But if she were a he—Christian instead of Christiana—those same professionals would instead most likely be thinking psychopath and not borderline.

promiscuity. Being overly dramatic or emotional and rapidly shifting emotions might represent having superficial emotions. And blaming others for failure or disappointment equates to not accepting responsibility.

It is not likely that people with psychopathy or almost psychopathy are being misdiagnosed with histrionic personality disorder. As with borderline personality disorder, clinical judgment is essential in making a diagnosis—merely checking off symptoms on a list is not enough. But the same considerations apply to both histrionic and borderline personality disorders: as in other psychological disorders, women may present differently than men. Future research will tell us just how accurate our current models of psychopathy are when applied to both sexes and whether we have an accurate sense of how prevalent psychopathy and almost psychopathy are across genders.

Anxiety Disorders

Exposure to extreme violence—experiencing it personally or witnessing it—can result in post-traumatic stress disorder (PTSD). PTSD is an anxiety disorder that is generally treatable with a combination of medication and psychotherapy. Individuals with PTSD may exhibit irritability and outbursts of anger, have difficulty forming meaningful relationships or experiencing loving feelings, and feel detached from others and emotionally numb. Once again, these symptoms could be mistaken for those of psychopathy, suggesting the presence of almost psychopathy in the absence of the full criteria. In combination with substance abuse, individuals with PTSD who have been exposed to severe trauma may be at increased risk for committing serious acts of violence.[34]

PTSD can be chronic, and when it stems from trauma that occurred earlier in life, it may look like a long-standing personality disorder. In fact, research has shown a high rate of childhood sexual abuse and physical abuse and neglect among patients with borderline personality disorder. PTSD symptoms that develop within the first month of a traumatic incident support a diagnosis of acute stress disorder; once those symptoms are present for a month, PTSD can be diagnosed. As such, changes in personality that mimic symptoms of psychopathy and develop within the months following a traumatic event should not be chalked up to the person being almost a psychopath. Also keep in mind that PTSD can have a delayed onset, presenting itself years after the initial trauma. Symptoms may occur spontaneously, in response to an additional traumatic event, or after exposure to a stimulus that revives memories of the trauma. As such, we must consider the diagnosis of delayed-onset PTSD when someone acutely develops irritability, outbursts of anger, alienation from loved ones, and emotional numbness after some major life event.

Substance Abuse

There is a good deal of overlap between substance abuse disorders and the social deviance elements of psychopathy. These can include a parasitic lifestyle, poor behavioral controls, promiscuity, impulsivity, irresponsibility, revocation of conditional release, and criminal versatility. While substance use disorders and psychopathy can occur together, disinhibition and impaired judgment due to the substance use may account for most of these behaviors. An important part of the differential diagnosis process is to determine if the substance use disorder is primary and if effective treatment would alleviate those behaviors that could contribute to a diagnosis of psychopathy. And if the only problem is substance abuse or dependence, many, if not all, of those behaviors could well be resolved through treatment.

* * *

Acute and long-term effects of toxins, bipolar disorder, major depression, PTSD, and substance use disorders are all amenable to treatment. That is less true for personality disorders and the following conditions that can cause certain symptoms resembling psychopathy. Generally, though, these conditions will not result in the full range of emotional and behavioral symptoms that define almost psychopathy.

Brain Injury

Some behaviors indicative of almost psychopathy, like impulsivity, reactive aggression, poor planning and organization, lack of empathy, and irresponsible behavior may develop in previously healthy individuals who have had brain injuries, primarily to the frontal lobes.[35] In their book *Psychiatric Aspects of Neurological Disease*, psychiatrist Dietrich Blumer and neurologist David Benson referred to this as *pseudopsychopathy*.[36] Damage to other areas of the brain, such as the amygdala, the anterior cingulate gyrus, and the temporal lobes, can also be associated with some symptoms of almost psychopathy and true psychopathy.

Asperger's Syndrome

Asperger's syndrome is a developmental disorder that affects a person's ability to socialize and communicate well with others and is one of the autism spectrum disorders. The symptoms of

Asperger's syndrome include these:

1. Engaging in one-sided, long-winded conversations without noticing whether the listener is engaged

2. Appearing not to empathize with or understand the feelings of others

3. Displaying unusual nonverbal communication, such as lack of eye contact and few facial expressions

4. Showing an intense obsession with one or two specific, narrow subjects

5. Having a hard time "reading" other people

6. Speaking in a voice that is monotonous, rigid, or unusually fast

7. Moving clumsily, with poor coordination[37]

Again, a major indicator of almost psychopathy is a distinct lack of empathy, and lack of empathy has traditionally been thought to be a hallmark of Asperger's syndrome. In fact, Asperger's syndrome is sometimes called *autistic psychopathy*. That is a misnomer. While both disorders involve inappropriate responses to the emotions of others, the cause of the dysfunction is different. And as researchers have shown, adolescent boys with autism spectrum disorders such as Asperger's have difficulty with the cognitive task of considering the perspective of another person, yet they experience real emotion and empathy for victims. Not so for those boys with psychopathic tendencies. In studies, they express less fear and less empathy than control subjects.[38]

People with Asperger's syndrome have an *impaired* understanding of other people's emotions due to difficulty interpreting verbal cues. They have a cognitive deficit that makes it more difficult for them to consider the perspective of another person. Any antisocial behavior they engage in is likely caused by an incorrect reading of the social situation. Their antisocial behaviors are not likely to be purposeful transgressions designed to give them some advantage. Almost psychopaths, on the other hand, may be perfectly capable of gauging the perspective of another, but they are not able to feel along with the other person. With psychopaths as with almost psychopaths, antisocial behavior frequently involves *intentional* manipulation and exploitation of others.

A 2010 study on social perception revealed a telling difference between the two disorders. Over 800 male and female study participants ranging in age from eighteen to seventy-three took a "Mind Survey," in which they were asked to judge the perceived experience and agency of nine entities (a baby, a dead woman, a dog, God, a man, a robot, Superman, a tree, and a woman). "Agency" and "experience" are related but distinct concepts: agency relates to whether the entity considered has the ability to plan, has memory, and can exercise self-control, while experience relates to whether the entity considered has the capacity for feeling pleasure, hunger, and fear. The participants also completed tests designed to measure three subclinical syndromes—autism spectrum disorder, schizotypy, and psychopathy. While all three disorders involve abnormalities in social interaction, they have distinct patterns of distorted perception (for our purposes, we are not going to cover schizotypy, which can involve magical thinking and delusions). Specifically, higher scores on the autism scale were linked to reduced perceptions of agency (whether the entities have the capacity to plan) in adult humans, suggesting that autism is linked with difficulty in understanding the goals of others. Higher scores on the psychopathy scale were associated with a decreased perception of experience (the capacity for pain and pleasure) in both humans and animals, which could help explain the cruel behavior typical of psychopaths; if those with elevated psychopathy scores don't "see" animals and other humans as experiencing pain, they may simply devalue both.[39]

. . .

One final comment about the differential diagnosis process. Although lists of symptoms help us narrow down the possible disorders causing the behavioral problems, as our descriptions of the various diagnoses illustrate in this chapter, the same symptoms may be present in multiple disorders. The challenge in making an accurate diagnosis is in recognizing the patterns of symptoms, how they fit together, and how the symptoms and the person who exhibits them respond to interventions. That takes clinical skill and experience, and so we again urge caution before you embark on using these lists to diagnose yourself or those around you.

Another Look at James

So what could be the problem with James from the last chapter? As we saw, James fell well short of meeting the criteria of a true psychopath. It appears that James falls into the almost psychopath realm, but to be more certain, let's turn to the differential diagnosis approach we talked about earlier and review the list of potential conditions that might cause the behaviors we see in James. If we can eliminate other potential causes for James's feelings and conduct, we can be more certain that James is an almost psychopath, with all that that implies. That, in turn, would suggest the appropriate strategies for dealing with James (or what to do if you *are* someone like James).

The first place to start is with a consideration of a specific medical diagnosis that might explain James's behaviors. James saw his primary care physician, who found no underlying medical conditions, including exposure to toxins (remember the professor and his cat!) that could be the cause of his behaviors at home, his infidelity, his personality traits, or his claimed depression.

Having ruled out an underlying medical condition, let's turn to the disorders that the *DSM–IV–TR* puts on what it calls Axis I. (See appendix B.) Is it possible that James's behavior all along was part of an underlying mood disorder, like major depression? Unlikely. Was James depressed? His claims of depressed mood, his failure to do the things he was asked to do, and occasionally sleeping the day away might all indicate that James was depressed. In fact, Carol had noticed that James seemed increasingly sad, but his mood had always lifted when she paid more attention to him. James told Carol he was "depressed" after she learned about his affair, and it is not clear whether his "depression" was due to a mood disorder or to having been caught. In any case, there were no indications at any other point in their marriage that he was suffering from any of the symptoms we just described. James is sad, perhaps, but not really suffering from diagnosable depression.

Bipolar disorder or the related cyclothymic disorder could account for James's mood complaints and variability in behavior, but he had no history of significant depression, cycling of moods, or manic or hypomanic states. As a result, they fall to the bottom of the list. In the absence of complaints or observations of anxiety symptoms, the anxiety disorders aren't part of the differential diagnosis.

As almost all of us know, alcohol and drugs can cause changes in behavior and emotions. And, to a large extent, that's their appeal. But there were no indications of substance abuse in James's case—he drank rarely and in a limited way, as he feared "getting fat," and his routine random drug testing at the fire department was always negative.

So we are left with James's reported depression that is more consistent with the sadness linked with some personality disorders, because it appears when James is lonely or feels that he is not getting sufficient admiration or attention. James's behaviors are also consistent with symptoms of a personality disorder.

Personality disorders (and personality traits) are coded on Axis II of the *DSM–IV–TR*. (Again, see appendix B.) As defined by the *DSM*, a personality disorder is "an enduring pattern of inner experience and behavior that deviates markedly from the expectations of the individual's culture, is pervasive and inflexible, has an onset in adolescence or early adulthood, is stable over time, and leads to distress or impairment." The personality disorders are divided into three clusters: A, B, and C. Cluster B contains the personality disorders most relevant to James's behaviors: antisocial, narcissistic, histrionic, and borderline.

Let's look at antisocial personality disorder first. The diagnostic criteria are in appendix A. With regard to the threshold criteria, it's true that James had a history of problem behavior before age fifteen, but he did not meet the criteria for conduct disorder, which according to the *DSM–IV–TR* requires "a repetitive and persistent pattern of behavior in which the basic rights of others or major age-appropriate societal norms or rules are violated," manifested by aggression to people or animals, destruction of property, deceitfulness or theft, or serious violation of rules.[40] James certainly had a pattern of lying, but primarily to Carol, and he did not meet any of the other criteria. So, while we may take a dim view of his infidelity, his lies, and his shirking of household chores, and we suspect that maybe he did take Carol's heirlooms from the house and may have been sneaking around at night, he doesn't meet the criteria for antisocial personality disorder.

But James comes closer to hitting the mark when it comes to the diagnostic criteria for narcissistic personality disorder. The need for constant attention and admiration, along with grandiosity about his skills and accomplishments, are some of those criteria. The disorder is named after the myth of Narcissus, the boy who fell in love with his own reflection and died of sorrow after realizing he could never obtain the object of his desire.

Consistent with the mythical Narcissus, people with this disorder are self-centered and self-absorbed; have unrealistically inflated views of their accomplishments, skills, or attractiveness; and crave admiration. Paradoxically, the condition is believed to arise from chronic low self-esteem and the need to prove their worth to themselves and others. These people may become depressed or enraged, possibly even violent, when they do not receive the admiration or credit they feel they deserve or when their self-doubts are confirmed by the criticism of others. Like psychopaths, they have a sense of entitlement and they exploit others. Unlike psychopaths, they may have a capacity for empathy, but that empathy gets turned off when they feel it necessary to fulfill their own needs.

The narcissistic personality style is common in our culture and may be a marker of success in many fields: our culture values self-confidence, assertiveness, and an ability to handle slights and setbacks even while being sensitive to them. But those factors can shift into narcissistic personality disorder when the self-confidence becomes arrogance, the assertiveness turns into a need to crush any competition, and the person is unable to tolerate not being the center of attention or being admired.

James has a need for admiration and has low tolerance for not being the center of attention; he also believes he is special, exhibits grandiosity and exaggerated self-importance, and is interpersonally exploitative—that is more than a personality style, but it gets him only four of the criteria, and five are needed for the diagnosis. As with psychopathy, a person doesn't need to meet the full criteria for a diagnosable disorder in order for his or her behaviors to be a problem. In this case, James might be diagnosed with "personality disorder not otherwise specified" (NOS) with antisocial and narcissistic traits. The NOS suffix to a diagnostic category indicates that the full criteria for a specific disorder are not met, but some elements of several diagnoses are present; for example, some but not all symptoms of antisocial and narcissistic personality disorder are found. Some clinicians might just list antisocial and narcissistic personality traits on Axis II. As previously noted, the upcoming fifth edition of the *DSM* will allow for a more nuanced, less categorical approach to diagnosing personality disorders. In fact, *DSM–V* may enable us to describe an individual's psycho-logical traits more specifically and get a better sense of whether people have a true mental disorder or are simply failing to balance their impulses, needs, and own standards of behavior—behavior that does not amount to a disorder. Has the dark side of their very human personalities gained a temporary advantage, or is it a way of life for them? If the former, there is cause for optimism. If the latter, we are in the realm of the almost psychopath, and there will be less chance of turning it around.

What Can Be Done?

No relationship, even those without challenges like James and Carol's, is free of conflict. Each member of the relationship brings emotional baggage to it, born of past experiences, genetic predispositions, and personality traits. The success or failure of any relationship is determined in large part by how well two people mesh in terms of what they bring to it and how they address conflict when it inevitably arises. A relationship between a more aggressive and assertive person and an easygoing, agreeable partner who avoids conflict at all costs, perhaps out of fear of angering the assertive partner, may have a worse prognosis than one in which both partners feel safe enough to stand their ground and work through the disagreement.

Were alternative outcomes possible in the saga of James and Carol? Perhaps, but not with any certainty. We're focusing on James in this chapter, so for simplicity's sake, let's just say that Carol is an average person, not perfect, but relatively free of behavioral quirks or unusual personality traits and with her own pet peeves. For example, when passive-aggressive behavior similar to what she experienced in an earlier relationship began to appear in James, it really got to her. She is hard working and likes to think the best of people—especially those she cares about. While she prefers to avoid conflict, she is willing to stand her ground when pushed beyond a certain point, as she did here.

What, if anything, could have been done? Should Carol have seen this coming? Hindsight, of course, is 20/20, and we can suggest that had she been paying attention, Carol could have put this all together and realized that James had some serious problems. As you read this story, somewhere along the way you may even have been saying to yourself (or Carol), "Get out! Now!"

We are very familiar with the problem of hindsight bias in both medicine and law. In medicine, we even have a special term for using hindsight and then criticizing others who failed to anticipate future events—the *retrospectoscope*, a fictional instrument that allows us to look back in time and always be correct in predicting future events. Worse still, a consultant or a malpractice attorney will come along and make a grand pronouncement about an unlikely clinical outcome that, now that it has occurred, was something that "anyone" could have predicted.

We won't fall into the trap of using the retrospectoscope and criticizing Carol's decisions. Love, after all, is blind (at least to a certain extent and for a limited time). Most people, thankfully, ride out the bumps in their relationships, ignore or quickly resolve what appear to be (and often are) minor problems, and live on contentedly. There may come a point, however, where minor problems, left unaddressed and unresolved, become too much or prove to represent a much more serious problem that cannot be ignored.

Without playing Monday morning quarterback to Carol

and James's relationship, let's look at some points where different decisions might have been made and what they were. We can divide the history of the relationship into two parts: before and after Carol opened the letter about James's affairs.

Prior to when Carol received that letter, a number of problematic events and behaviors occurred, all of which should have been handled with a basic rule in mind: the more people can talk with their partners about the things that bother them, the healthier the relationship will be. James's dependency, his sulking when he felt ignored, his self-centered behavior, his comments to friends that Carol found disturbing, his failure to fulfill his promises to do household chores, and his rapid return to baseline behavior after promising it would not happen again—all of these ideally would have been addressed directly and discussed openly by the couple. It would have been even more important, but even more difficult, for Carol to talk with her husband about the newfound information she received from James's family about his past.

What we're suggesting here is not easy. Every one of us has bitten our tongues rather than speak our minds when troubled by a partner's comment or behavior, chalking it up to a bad day or a simple misunderstanding, rather than enter into a difficult conversation. And that is often the right decision, at least temporarily, so long as problems don't mount as they did for Carol.

Let's say that Carol did speak up when she noticed James's troubling behaviors and attitudes. Would it have made a difference to the outcome, given James's personality traits? Maybe. Here's how: By expressing concerns about small events like this, especially early in the relationship and in a calm and conversational manner, a couple does several things. First, the partners get practice dealing with conflict over relatively small issues. Second, the person expressing concern gets experience in speaking up and overcoming the anxiety that comes with starting what could be an unpleasant discussion. Third, the partner who is receiving the comments has the experience of hearing a criticism or complaint from a loved one—never pleasant—but in a way that feels safe, because it is not an attack on him or her as a person, but an effort to solve a problem that they share in the relationship. Having practiced on the small stuff, they should find the bigger conflicts easier to handle. Conversely, if the concerns are raised in "attack" rather than problem-solving mode, or if the reaction to an expressed concern is aggressive denial, reciprocal blame, or outright rejection of the concern, you can be sure that the odds of any future efforts will be greatly reduced for all but the most stalwart of partners.

Simple, right? Of course not. Even the most intelligent, rational, loving, even-tempered person can have trouble expressing concerns to a loved one or hearing such concerns. And the toughest part of addressing issues such as those Carol faced is often taking that deep breath and starting the conversation. Even then, the process can run into challenges. People can lose their tempers, get anxious, feel attacked, and lash back—look at James's response when Carol asked him about the treatment he said he was getting. A person hearing a concern expressed by a loved one may readily apologize out of fear of abandonment, to escape from the discussion, or for a number of other reasons—only to later resent the criticism and then backslide. That may have been what was going on with James and his behavior that Carol felt was passive aggressive.

There are techniques for optimizing the chances of success in these encounters that are beyond the scope of what we are discussing here. Along those lines, we recommend *Difficult Conversations: How to Discuss What Matters Most*, by Douglas Stone, Bruce Patton, Sheila Heen, and Roger Fisher (who are part of Harvard Law School and the Harvard Negotiation Project), which contains valuable information about addressing conflict at home and at work.

Let's assume that Carol works up the courage and addresses her concerns with James, that he does have these narcissistic personality traits, and that the conversations do not bring about the hoped-for changes. What solutions are available? Both couples therapy and individual therapy have a role in situations like this. It's important to keep in mind that there are different types or modalities of psychotherapy, such as individual, couples, group, and family, as well as many different types or schools of psychotherapy. Which one is the best for a given situation depends on the people involved. Regardless of the type of therapy, the keys to successful therapy usually include a patient who is willing to try to address his or her problems and a knowledgeable, compassionate therapist who is dedicated to helping solve those problems in a professional manner.

Couples therapy makes sense, as the relationship itself has a problem in terms of communication. A couples therapist can be thought of as a therapist for the relationship, hearing out both partners and encouraging them to express their feelings and perspectives. The therapy can provide an opportunity to resolve the conflict and to strengthen the relationship for the future.

Individual therapy can be useful for narcissistic personality disorder, and even more so for narcissistic traits. The higher functioning the person is, the more likely treatment will be helpful. The therapy usually focuses on the person's underlying low self-esteem and fear of imperfection, with a goal of gaining self-acceptance and reining in the grandiosity and animosity to authority. Group therapy, in which the person receives feedback from peers and hears the experiences of others, can be especially helpful. It is highly likely that James was not even aware of his own pattern of behaviors or why it was so distressing to Carol. Assuming a willing patient with some capacity for insight, psychotherapy (both individual and group) can help people become aware of what they are doing and why and can potentially lead to real behavior change.

If James had gotten into treatment, and Carol and James had done some couples work, there might—*might*—have been a different outcome. That is even more likely if the interventions had helped James stay faithful to Carol. Relationships can survive infidelity, but combined with Carol's past concerns, James's newly revealed history of behavioral problems, his denial of the affairs, and then his lies about treatment, it all may have proven to be too much.

Perhaps this relationship was bound to end. In any case, help is available to individuals who exhibit these behaviors and to couples that encounter such difficulties. Hope lies in actively addressing concerns as they arise. The risk of a negative outcome simply increases when concerns are allowed to fester and become bigger problems.

■ ◆ ■

Part 2

Dealing with Almost Psychopaths in Our Lives

| 5 |

Living with an Almost Psychopath

Conflicts in a relationship can take on many forms, but the most problematic is when one spouse abuses the other—verbally, psychologically, or physically. Such abuse knows no social class or educational barriers, as our next case example shows.

Lucas

Professor Lucas Spencer was fifty years old and a well-regarded academic at a major university. He and his wife, Jenny, lived in a wealthy suburb where they had raised their two bright and accomplished children. To the outside world, Lucas, Jenny, and their children seemed to be a thriving, happy family. Between his teaching, consulting work, and income from several patents he held, Lucas brought in a substantial income, and Jenny didn't have to work; actually, Lucas insisted that she not have a job. Although Jenny had a degree in art and had always dreamed of pursuing a career in photography, Lucas saw it as his duty to provide for the family, and he made sure that Jenny knew and agreed with his view.

Lucas and Jenny had met twenty-five years ago; he was beginning his second year of graduate school, and she was working at a coffee shop near his apartment to make ends meet until her artistic career got going. Jenny was pleasant, attractive in an artsy sort of way, and after several weeks of flirting and chatting, became interested in Lucas, his work, and his opinions. While he plainly preferred that they talk about him and his projects, he enjoyed looking at her photographs and managed to express interest in her daily activities. Lucas was soon infatuated with Jenny, wanting to be with her every minute. Worried that she might lose interest when they were apart, Lucas became frustrated when she had to work an extra shift or could not go out because she was working on a new set of prints.

For her part, Jenny was flattered by Lucas's attention and charmed by his desire to be with her all the time; no one had ever been so intensely interested in her before. Within months, the two were nearly inseparable, and they decided to move into one apartment just as Lucas was finishing up his thesis. As soon as he got his first faculty appointment, which was offered to him even before he finished defending his thesis, Lucas asked Jenny to marry him. She accepted.

While they initially talked about her photography and plans for a gallery, Lucas quickly shifted to pressing his wife to stay at home, raise the children they planned to have, and play the role of dutiful faculty spouse. He was far more concerned with his traditional values than with Jenny's feelings about her own career. Seeing this as the sort of compromise people make in marriage, Jenny complied with Lucas's wishes. Besides, Lucas reassured her that "someday" she could set up a studio. Nevertheless, she was left with the uneasy feeling that instead of working together, she had been pressured into giving in through a combination of Lucas's emotional fervor and her own concerns about being a "good wife."

Over time, Jenny's real role in the marriage became crystal clear; she was to support Lucas in his career, arrange dinner parties for his faculty colleagues and consulting clients, and keep him from being burdened by household and childcare worries. Lucas continued to give lip service to the idea of Jenny spending time on her photography, but he never agreed to any of the steps that could actually make this happen. He didn't share any of the household responsibilities and couldn't quite see his way to agreeing to hire any help for Jenny. But Jenny was determined, and between grocery shopping, cleaning, decorating, and changing diapers, she slowly managed to build her portfolio. For reasons she did not quite understand, she kept the extent of her photography work secret from her husband; all he knew was that she still took some "snapshots" (as he called them) from time to time. But keeping up with her photography became increasingly difficult as Lucas made more and more requests of her—special meals, dinner parties for colleagues, ironing his shirts, and so on.

The one thing Lucas did take responsibility for was the household finances. Citing how he had grown up in a poor family, he asked Jenny to indulge his desire to be on top of all the financial decisions, pay the bills, and manage the family budget. In this way, even early in the marriage, Lucas further established his control over Jenny's life. Not only was she to stay at home, but she was given a set allowance for the household expenses. And, at Lucas's insistence, they had a set time— the first Sunday of every month—to review expenditures, although over time Lucas asked to look at the numbers more often. This meant that Jenny had to keep track of all of her receipts or be able to retrieve the information electronically. These meetings always made Jenny anxious, as Lucas would take on a patronizing, scolding tone if he found what he considered to be excessive expenditures. Her anxiety extended to every shopping trip she made, as she approached everything in terms of "What would Lucas say if he saw the receipt?"

Stopping her from working and watching every penny weren't Lucas's only methods of dominating Jenny's life. While the children were young, Jenny's friends were other mothers she met through the children's school-related activities. On the few occasions when she got together with these friends, Lucas would later ask detailed questions about what they did, where they went, and what they talked about—to the point where she took no pleasure in these outings and stopped accepting invitations.

Despite years of having her own wishes stifled, Jenny hadn't entirely given up on Lucas or the marriage. She sometimes tried to engage Lucas in serious conversations about current events. His reaction? He generally ignored her; on the rare occasions that he listened, he was plainly exasperated by what he considered her unsophisticated views. If she participated in intellectual conversations when they were with friends, he would find a way to put her down. On one occasion, after a colleague of his commented on Jenny's knowledge of current events and the arts, Lucas asked her when they got home, "Why would he think you were smart?" When friends expressed an interest in her photography, Lucas would pretend to be supportive, even implying that it was thanks to him that she was again working on her art. After such social events, where Jenny was the center of attention and not him, Lucas would become sullen and irritable.

Once the children went off to college, Jenny lost even the limited school-related social contacts she had and began feeling more isolated than ever before. To fill the void, she turned more openly to her photography and began bringing her portfolio to local art galleries, where it attracted some attention. Seeing that he couldn't force Jenny to give up her photography, Lucas set about minimizing the significance of her efforts and the quality of her work, in contrast to what he viewed as "real" art. When they were with others, he made snide comments about Jenny's "hobby," suggesting that she was a suburban housewife suffering from empty nest syndrome and that this gave her something useful to do when she wasn't watching soap operas.

As Jenny began to expand her horizons through her photography, Lucas again figured out a way to exert dominion over her life; he began keeping track of the odometer readings on her car. Claiming that it was an environmental and economic issue, he insisted that Jenny keep a log of where she went each day. Initially, he reviewed the mileage on a weekly basis, comparing the odometer readings to the number of gallons printed on the receipt from the gas pump. On an occasion when Jenny forgot to print the receipt at the pump, Lucas berated her for being irresponsible. Didn't she care about the environment? Or how expensive gasoline had become? After that, Lucas began monitoring the mileage each day, asking Jenny where she had gone and checking the mileage against Google Maps.

One day, Lucas became very agitated when Jenny's answer

about her whereabouts that day didn't satisfy his curiosity. He pointed out that even separate trips to the local big box store and the grocery store would not have required that much driving. Lucas insisted on knowing exactly where she had gone, repeating the question over and over again while moving continually closer to where she sat. Jenny felt both physically and psychologically intimidated; she sensed that Lucas knew she wasn't telling him everything. But she couldn't tell him the truth: she had taken a side trip to visit an old friend from college to talk about her growing concern with Lucas's controlling ways, her sense of isolation, and her inability to work on her photography without feeling harassed by him. Jenny began to stammer, overwhelmed by her efforts to explain herself, her guilt at having doubts about the marriage and having broken the implicit "rules" in their relationship. She was afraid of Lucas and his growing anger, and confused by how she could have ended up in this situation.

As she struggled to explain what had happened, Lucas erupted, grabbed a glass vase that had been a wedding gift from one of her friends, and smashed it to the floor. As he did so, he yelled at her that if she ever lied to him again, "something other than glass is going to get broken." Jenny sobbed an apology. Later that evening, with Jenny still crying, Lucas went to her and apologized, promising that it would never happen again. He only asked that she be honest with him about where she was and what she was doing, because "Trust is so important in a marriage."

Nothing changed. Lucas, now even more suspicious of Jenny, increased his scrutiny of her every move, made more demands, and isolated her further from her few social contacts.

He tightened his financial control and became increasingly critical of her housekeeping and cooking.

A month or so after breaking the vase, Lucas became enraged when dinner was both late and overcooked. He threw his plate across the table and knocked over his chair as he stood up and charged at Jenny, pinning her against the wall and screaming in her face. She began to cry, and as Lucas loosened his grip on her, she slipped away. Jenny grabbed the car keys as she ran out the door, then drove to her college friend's house and told her what Lucas had just done. This friend, and others, had always been somewhat concerned about Lucas and how he spoke to Jenny. But she had seemed happy, so they had not said anything. Lucas called Jenny on her cell phone, asking for forgiveness and promising that it would never happen again. Jenny felt the urge to give in, but her friend insisted that she get some advice from a local social service agency that worked with victims of domestic violence. Instead of going home, Jenny called the police and told the officer that she felt physically threatened by Lucas. Jenny declined to press charges, although she did get a temporary restraining order. Deciding that she needed to be away from Lucas, she made arrangements to pack up her things and move to her parents' house when she knew Lucas would be away from home for a few afternoons. Through a local domestic violence program, she entered into therapy and began the long and difficult process of extricating and protecting herself from Lucas.

A Pervasive Problem

Domestic violence—now also referred to as intimate partner violence (IPV) to include the wider range of relationships recognized by society—continues to be a major problem in the United States and elsewhere in the world. The American Medical Association defines *intimate partner violence* as "a pattern of coercive behaviors that may include repeated battering and injury, psychological abuse, sexual assault, progressive social isolation, deprivation, and intimidation." In 2011, the Centers for Disease Control and Prevention released the National Intimate Partner Violence Survey (which was based on interviews with over 16,000 adults), and the data are startling:

- Nearly 1 in 5 women, and 1 in 71 men, have been raped (completed or attempted forced penetration or alcohol/drug-facilitated completed penetration) at some point in their lives, with more than half of female victims of rape reporting that they were raped by an intimate partner and more than half of male victims reporting that they were raped by an acquaintance.

- About 1 in 4 women, and 1 in 7 men, have suffered severe physical violence by an intimate partner (such as being hit with a fist or beaten) at some point in their lifetime.

- Nearly half of all women and men in the United States have experienced psychological aggression by an intimate partner during their lifetime.

- About 1 in 6 women, and 1 in 19 men, have been stalked at some point during their lifetime, with 60 percent of women and 40 percent of men having been stalked by a current or former intimate partner.[41]

While both men and women commit intimate partner violence, they do not do so in the same way or to the same degree.

Some studies have indicated that men and women are equally likely to resort to low levels of violence, with severe violence more likely to be used by men—especially those with criminal backgrounds, severe psychological distress, or certain personality traits. And intimate partner violence perpetrated by men rather than women is more likely to result in severe physical injury.[42]

Intimate partner violence knows no social, economic, or ethnic barriers—it's a problem found in the inner city, suburbs, and rural areas. It affects the poor, the middle class, and the wealthy. A 2011 study at two orthopedic fracture clinics in Canada found that women who screened positive for intimate partner violence spanned a wide array of ages, ethnic groups, and levels of education and income.[43] A screener for the study obtained background information from people who agreed to participate and then gave them an anonymous questionnaire that directly asked if the participant's partner had abused her physically, emotionally, or sexually over the past year. The participants were also asked to complete two more extensive questionnaires: the Woman Abuse Screening Tool and the Partner Violence Screen. The results of this study—that over 30 percent of the women who went to the fracture clinics had experienced intimate partner violence at some time during the preceding year, with 8.5 percent experiencing physical abuse—are interesting, especially compared to the prior beliefs of those who presumably wind up treating many of the female victims of intimate partner violence—the orthopedic surgeons of Canada. A 2008 survey of nearly two hundred of Canada's orthopedic surgeons revealed that the vast majority of participants (87 percent) believed that less than 1 percent of their patients suffered from intimate partner violence. The remaining respondents believed that the prevalence of intimate partner violence in their practice was between 5 and 10 percent.

Another study on the potential causes of ongoing IPV by men against female partners examined the possible roles played by the perpetrators' antisocial traits, attitudes and values, and substance use; the characteristics of the relationship as well as that of their neighborhood; and the couple's socioeconomic status. Among all of these factors, the study found that the perpetrator's antisocial traits, especially psychopathy, had the strongest causal connection.[44] There is evidence, however, that financial hardship does increase the risk of intimate partner violence.[45]

It's More Than Physical Abuse

The common perception that IPV always involves physical attacks (the kind that send women to orthopedic fracture clinics) is far too limited to account for the extent and scope of abuse that occurs in some intimate relationships. As the American Medical Association's definition indicates, IPV also includes sexual assault, psychological violence, and intimidation. And it turns out that subclinical psychopathy is associated with a wide range of risky and violent sexual behaviors and strongly negative attitudes toward partners in relationships.

In a 2005 study, 612 undergraduates in Canada took part in a self-report study regarding their attitudes and behaviors. Researchers were interested in learning about any influences of psychopathic traits and behaviors on the students' intimate relationships. The participants were all enrolled in a first-year psychology class at a large university and received course credit for taking part in the study. Approximately 75 percent of the participants were female, and the mean age was 19.8 years.

The students were given a package of self-report questionnaires and were told not to put any identifying information anywhere on the questionnaires. One part of the package was a forty-four-item version of the Self-Report Psychopathy Scale (SRP–III, modeled after Hare's PCL–R). Students were asked to respond to statements such as "I have shoplifted" and "I find it easy to manipulate people" by placing them along a scale, with 1 indicating "strongly disagree" and 5 indicating "strongly agree." Other parts of the package were self-report questionnaires designed to measure risky and violent behaviors and relationship attitudes. (These screens included the Violence Assessment Index, the Aggressive Sexual Behavior Inventory, the HIV/AIDS Risk Behavior Form, the Rape Supportive Attitude Scales, the Perceived Relationship Quality Component, and the Relationship Questionnaire.) The final part of the questionnaire looked at infidelity, using as the measures the HMP Attraction Survey, the Anonymous Romantic Attraction Survey, and the Sociosexual Orientation Inventory.

The study showed that those with higher scores on the SRP–III (the psychopathy scale) were more likely to engage in risky sexual behaviors and obtain sex by coercion, including physical and verbal aggression and even the use of drugs. They were also found to be continuously pursuing short-term sexual encounters with little or no regard for whether their targets were already in relationships. Overall, it appears that those who had elevations on the SRP-III—the almost psychopaths—tended to exhibit and use manipulation and aggression in their intimate relationships. Those who would qualify for almost psychopath status also tended to report negative feelings toward relationships and a dismissive attachment style. Most chilling, those in the almost psychopath range were more accepting of rape myths and were found to have more pro-rape attitudes than the general population.[46]

The take-away from this research: as they are with the rest of the world, so they are even with intimate partners; the relationships of almost psychopaths are very likely to be filled with mistrust, manipulation, coercion, and intimidation.

Intimate Partner Violence and True Psychopaths

While intimate partner violence can occur as a single, isolated event, more often it is part of a pattern of disturbing behaviors. It appears that some subtypes of men—such as those who are violent, antisocial/psychopathic/borderline, or are experiencing significant psychological distress—are most likely to progress from single instances of low-level intimate partner violence to what has been termed *intimate terrorism.*[47] The research is quite clear that intimate partner violence is a prime area for encountering either full-fledged psychopaths or those who almost meet the criteria.

Let's look at an example of a full-fledged psychopath who engaged in verbal and emotional abuse, as well as actual physical violence and recurrent death threats.

Jamaal

Jamaal was incarcerated for violating a permanent restraining order that prohibited him from having any contact with his wife, let alone making death threats as he had in the past. The judge who had issued the order decided that Jamaal needed some time behind bars after he repeatedly ignored the judge's warnings and orders.

Jamaal had physically assaulted his wife, Mary, on numerous occasions, after which she would get temporary restraining orders—court orders directing Jamaal to stay away from Mary and have no contact with her. As the name indicates, temporary restraining orders, commonly issued in intimate partner violence situations, are temporary; they are meant to provide immediate, short-term stability and safety in what are often volatile, fast-moving circumstances. The idea is that if conditions warrant it and the victim makes the request, the order can become permanent or at least be extended. However, as frequently happens in intimate partner violence cases, Jamaal would offer profuse apologies and promise that it would never happen again, and so Mary never applied to make the restraining orders permanent.

After seeing Jamaal one too many times, the judge issued a permanent restraining order, warning Jamaal that violation of this one would earn him a stay in a correctional facility. Sure enough, Jamaal was back in court a month later—he had gone to the apartment where Mary was living, they got in an argument in which she claimed he threatened her, and she called the police. Before the judge, Jamaal claimed that he never threatened Mary and that she was making this up. He also claimed that Mary had invited him over for dinner and to spend the night, which Mary acknowledged was true. The judge pointed out that Jamaal had violated *his* order—this had nothing to do with Mary, and she had no authority to give Jamaal permission to violate the judge's order. He admonished Mary for this and then sent Jamaal off to the correctional facility, where he was evaluated as part of a research project on psycho-pathology and domestic violence.

Jamaal's score on the PCL–R? He was well into the psy-chopathy range. A violent gang member in his youth, a drug dealer and burglar with grandiose notions of his talents, and a substance abuser, Jamaal had been supported by multiple women, all of whom he treated badly and for whom he had no empathy.

One of the first things Jamaal did after being released was to go to a pay phone, call Mary, and threaten to kill her for sending him away to prison. Mary, having received some good counseling and support in the meantime, called the police, and Jamaal was immediately arrested. As luck would have it, Jamaal ended up before the same judge, who this time sentenced him to a much longer term of incarceration.

The Differences between Lucas and Jamaal

Jamaal was a full-blown psychopath. But what about Lucas? Is he in the same category as Jamaal? Is there any hope for him mending his ways? Let's start with the psychopathy question. Lucas was certainly never a drug-dealing (or drug-using) gang member. In fact, he had never been charged with, let alone convicted of, a crime. He was meticulous about following rules, he was honest (for the most part) on his taxes, and friends and neighbors regarded him as an upright citizen. But he did have troublesome personality traits: irritability, a short temper, arrogance and a sense of entitlement, a deep-seated fear of abandonment, a lack of empathy for how his behavior affected others, a need for total control, and a lack of insight into his own behavior.

Lucas's distinctive personality traits, especially his bullying and need to control others, began early in life. A self-described nerd in high school, Lucas had a limited number of friends and a virtually nonexistent social life during most of his school years. He was not so much a class clown as he was a wise guy—frequently using his superior intelligence to make sarcastic, cutting comments about others. These comments would draw laughs, but they had an angry, nasty edge. Big enough to be intimidating, especially when angry, Lucas was not challenged when he bullied schoolmates, which he did both intellectually and physically.

Lucas's anger mimicked what he saw at home, where his parents drank heavily and fought frequently, both verbally and physically. They had little time for Lucas and his two younger brothers, all of whom were often left to fend for themselves. The scant attention Lucas and his siblings did get from their parents was anything but nurturing and was usually abusive. In spite of the chaos at home, Lucas did extremely well academically and went on to earn his undergraduate degree and PhD at two of the most prestigious universities in the world.

Relieved to be away from home, Lucas was more socially active than he had been throughout high school, but none of his romantic relationships lasted more than a few months. There was a pattern in these relationships, a pattern that was later replicated with Jenny. After quickly becoming infatuated, Lucas would completely throw himself at the woman of the moment, wanting to be together all the time, and wanting—needing, actually—to know where she was and what she was doing when they were apart. Some of the young women he pursued found this romantic. But that would change as Lucas went beyond this "crush" behavior by insisting that the girl-friend of the moment be in constant contact and by becoming extremely jealous when she was with other friends, male or female.

Eventually, the darker side of Lucas's "devotion" would surface, as it later would with Jenny. He would lose his temper and become physically threatening when his needs for reassurance and constant attention were not met. Although he never hit any of the women, he was still intimidating. After venting his anger, Lucas would apologize profusely, send flowers and gifts, and beg forgiveness, explaining that his outburst was just the result of the depth of his love or the stress of school or both. And Lucas really believed that was the case, although a part of him enjoyed his ability to control these women through a combination of physical intimidation and persuasion. Eventually, each of these women left without looking back—not that Lucas made it easy for them; in at least one case, a former girl-friend transferred to another school to get away from him.

By the end of his junior year, Lucas's reputation had spread around campus and no one would date him. Perplexed, he saw a therapist at the college counseling center and explained how he quickly became deeply attached to women and could easily become overwhelmingly upset when he felt he was being ignored or, worse yet, rejected. He minimized the anger he had shown and did not mention that the women were frightened of him. The counselor suggested that his attachment to these women was a bit premature and that he would benefit from slowing things down a bit and being less intense. "Got it," Lucas said to himself. What he "got" was that his technique had to change, not that his underlying attitude or verbal and physical behaviors were inappropriate. Lucas decided to back away from dating his senior year, concentrated on his honors thesis, and then accepted an offer to go to a top graduate school on the other side of the country. A new place and a fresh start.

Lucas did outstanding work in graduate school, was recognized as one of the rising stars in his field, and completed his thesis in record time. He was admired but intensely disliked by his fellow graduate students, who regarded him as arrogant and unkind. For his part, Lucas felt intensely lonely. He hesitated to date, still feeling hurt and confused about his social problems in college, and he had no insight into why his classmates seemed to resent him so.

Is Lucas a Psychopath?

The backstory on Lucas pretty much takes psychopathy off the table. Yes, there is callousness and lack of empathy and a tendency to be manipulative. But his sense of intellectual self-worth was not grandiose—it was in keeping with the feedback he had gotten all his life. If we were to run through the formal diagnostic criteria of psychopathy, we would find that Lucas is not a psychopath (although you probably don't feel a great deal of sympathy for him).

A Differential Look

Let's look at the differential diagnosis, starting, as we always should, with underlying reversible medical disorders that either may be directly causing his behavior or may be exacerbating underlying conditions. In looking for acute medical conditions that are a possible primary cause for his abusive dynamic with Jenny, we are immediately struck by the fact that these behaviors aren't new. He displayed the same pattern of behavior in other relationships during college, and it seems that how he interacted with Jenny was a logical extension of those earlier patterns in the context of a long marriage.

But there does seem to be evidence of a *worsening* of Lucas's behavior, and in medicine, it's fairly common to have two conditions at once—he could have his preexisting problems and then something new that makes the prior behavior even more pronounced or problematic. In light of this possibility, it would be appropriate to make sure Lucas has a thorough evaluation. Acknowledging that these are not new behaviors, our focus in ruling out underlying medical problems would be on those conditions that can exacerbate preexisting behaviors. The list would include, but not be limited to these:

1. Space occupying lesions of the brain, such as benign and malignant tumors
2. Dementia due to vascular disease, multiple small infarcts (strokes), Alzheimer's disease, or other dementing illnesses
3. Cancers of various types
4. Blood disorders, including anemia
5. Endocrine disorders, such as diabetes or thyroid disease
6. Toxins (remember the professor and the tick powder?)
7. New onset of symptoms of mental illness, including
   a. Hypomania or mania
   b. Major depression
   c. Substance abuse
   d. Delusional disorder, especially jealous type[††]
8. Midlife crisis

Lucas had gotten a clean bill of health from his primary care physician a week before the final incident with Jenny—no diabetes or other endocrine problems, no cancer, and no blood disorders. But the doctor did not know Lucas had any behavioral issues ("Everything is great at home, as usual. Jenny's a doll and keeps herself busy taking pictures," he told his doctor) and so would have no reason to look more closely for causes of problematic behaviors. Let's run through some of these possible conditions that deserve closer scrutiny:

- **Dementia.** Dementing illnesses, whatever their cause, usually develop slowly. The first sign of their presence may be a change in personality—often a worsening of negative preexisting personality traits. Verbal and social skills are generally the last to deteriorate, and intelligent people can appear cognitively intact and behave quite normally even after a dementia has begun. Ron has evaluated numerous people with advanced dementia who carried on pleasant, coherent conversations—so long as they were not pressed to remember specific dates or facts,

---

†† A delusion is an unshakable false belief, inconsistent with the belief of a person's culture, that is held in the face of what is ordinarily considered convincing evidence to the contrary and that is not caused by an underlying medical condition or effect of a substance. Delusional disorder is a mental illness in which a person has one or more nonbizarre delusions, that is, they could possibly happen, such as being followed, being poisoned, or having an illness. In "delusional disorder, jealous type," the person holds a delusional belief that his or her partner is having an affair with one or more other people. As with other delusions, any shred of evidence is viewed as supporting the belief, including protests to the contrary. These disorders are particularly hard to treat, in part because the affected person denies that there is anything wrong with him or her. In addition, such delusions respond poorly to antipsychotic medications that may be more effective against delusions associated with other psychotic disorders such as schizophrenia. When a delusion does resolve, the patient often says that its substance has resolved— the FBI is no longer conducting surveillance, for example—but still believes that it occurred in the past.

like where they were born—or who behaved as if Ron were an old acquaintance, even though they had never met before. Lucas is not too young to be showing early signs of dementia.

- **Toxins.** Again, seeing no signs of cognitive decline and unaware of any behavior problems, Lucas's primary care physician would have had no reason to screen for heavy metal contamination, such as lead. We know of one case where a college-educated man, something of a do-it-yourselfer, developed profound behavioral changes including impulsivity, poor judgment, irritability, and failing memory. The culprit was lead. He had invented what he felt was a better coffeepot, which he made himself—using lead-based solder to assemble the device. His astute physician came up with a differential diagnosis and through some medical detective work identified the source. After a course of chelation therapy (chelating agents bind with the metal and allow the offending substance to be eliminated from the body) and a switch to a commercial coffeepot, he did quite well. And of course, there is always the question of insecticides and other household poisons.

- **Hypomania and mania.** As noted earlier, symptoms can include irritability, impulsivity, and irresponsibility. It is unlikely to present for the first time at age fifty, and Lucas had no earlier signs or symptoms.

- **Major depression.** This common mood disorder can present somewhat differently in men than women, often because men are either poor at identifying their emotions or ashamed to talk about them. It can also lead to irritability, poor judgment, indifference to the feelings and needs of others, and a general sense of unhappiness that spills into and gets acted out upon in relationships. Lucas is at a prime age for new-onset major depression, so this would need to be screened for carefully.

- **Substance abuse.** Most substances of abuse and alcohol most commonly, can cause loss of impulse control, impaired judgment, and irritability. Alcohol, in particular, is on the list of problem substances to screen for.

- **Delusional disorder.** This is part of the differential diagnosis, and the key would be to distinguish between overly controlling behavior and possessiveness and a deeply held belief that Jenny was cheating on him.

In fact, Lucas's behavior cannot be chalked up to any of these potentially underlying diagnoses—no dementia, depression, mania, or psychosis, and no toxins, including alcohol and drugs. Rather, his behavior is the result of long-standing borderline and narcissistic personality traits that rise to the level of a personality disorder, now exacerbated by the stress of a midlife crisis.

Most of us have a general sense what *midlife* crisis means, even without knowing the precise definition. This term has grown quite popular since it was introduced by Elliott Jacques in 1965.[48] The basic idea comes from the understanding that human development continues beyond childhood and throughout adult life. Adult development, like child development, has certain key transition points. For men, as well as women, this can include the point at which the children have been raised and have moved on to their own adult lives, careers have plateaued or begun to decline, and people realize that they are on the "down" slope of the life cycle. This can trigger depression, but it can also lead to an existential crisis: What has this all been about? What have I accomplished? Which of my goals have I met? Where have I failed? And for a person predisposed by personality and life experiences, the fear and anxiety associated with this may be taken out on others.[49]

As mentioned earlier, personality traits tend to get exacerbated under stress, including illness. A number of personality traits and disorders have been associated with physically aggressive domestic violence/intimate partner violence perpetrated by males. In the 1990s, Amy Holtzworth-Munroe and Gregory L. Stuart developed a typology of domestic violence offenders, describing them along three dimensions: severity of violence, generality of violence, and personality disorder or psychopathology. They found that these dimensions differentiated among three batterer types: family only, generally violent/ antisocial, and dysphoric/borderline.[50] This last group of violent men is characterized by extreme psychological distress and evidence of borderline personality traits.

The family-only batterers (the group that Lucas belongs in) show low severity of violence, low generality of violence, low criminal involvement, low to moderate depression and alcohol abuse, and moderate levels of anger. In addition to engaging in less frequent and severe violence, individuals in this group tend to have more positive views of women, less severe psychopathology, and more limited problems with attachment than the other groups, but they may also be overdependent on and preoccupied with their partner. Those who are preoccupied have been described as having a negative self-image and being insecure in close relationships, often being jealous and possessive.

Offenders in the dysphoric/borderline group, people with depressed mood and characteristics of borderline personality disorder, had moderate to high marital violence, violence outside the family, criminal involvement, and a tendency toward borderline or schizoidal personality, moderate alcohol abuse, and high levels of depression and anger. The generally violent/antisocial offenders had moderate to high levels of violence, high levels of violence outside the family, criminal involvement and antisocial personality characteristics, high levels of alcohol abuse, moderate anger levels, and low levels of depression.[51]

Building on the work of Holtzworth-Munroe and Stuart, in 2006, Rebecca Johnson and colleagues studied men convicted of domestic violence crimes in England. They identified four subtypes of offenders: low pathology, borderline, antisocial, and narcissistic.[52] The majority—remember, this was a study of those with criminal convictions for domestic violence—fell into the generally violent/antisocial group. Less research has been done on female perpetrators; research has instead focused on the personality traits of female victims of domestic abuse.

In a twenty-year study, Miriam K. Ehrensaft and colleagues demonstrated how early life experiences affect the risk of being a perpetrator of domestic violence in adulthood. Along with conduct disorder in adolescence (which conferred the highest risk), exposure to family violence between parents and excessive punishment or punishment aimed at asserting authority over children are associated with increased risk of partner violence in adulthood.[53]

Lucas appears to fall into that group of men who engage in intimate partner violence and who are characterized not by antisocial/violent behavior outside the family, but rather by intrafamilial violence alone, likely resulting from poor attachment to their parents in childhood, negative emotions about themselves and others, and borderline personality traits.[54] While he is not a true psychopath, Lucas's situation sounds pretty grim. Can anything be done? In the United States, treatment programs for batterers have become extremely popular, especially as court-ordered treatment in criminal cases and sometimes even in civil family law cases. Doubt has been cast on the effectiveness of those programs by a number of studies, but alternative intervention programs have fared no better.[55] Jenny would be ill-advised to return to the relationship, having already experienced his long-standing controlling behavior, emotional and verbal abuse, and physically threatening behavior. Maybe, with significant psychotherapy and even more significant motivation to change, Lucas might come to understand his behavior and what it is about. Whether that will be enough to bring about fundamental change is another question. But since he's fifty, we're not overly optimistic. As noted earlier, if Lucas were a psychopath, antidepressant medication might improve his impulsivity and aggressiveness—even if he is not clinically depressed—but it could also increase his ability to manipulate others.[56]

Jenny, on the other hand, would benefit from seeing a therapist familiar with relationship issues, especially those involving intimate partner violence. She will need support in understanding that she was not at fault for what she experienced or for the end of the marriage. Victims of intimate partner violence often blame themselves, feel sorry for their partners, who they believe acted out of weakness, and return to them out of a sense of compassion and commitment. Friends, family, and clinicians may struggle to understand why the battered partner would return to the relationship. Conversely, unless the violence is severe and obvious, family members and friends may not understand the need to leave the relationship, and so end up withholding much-needed support. Psychological, verbal, and emotional abuse—and even physical abuse —that takes place behind closed doors may not be known to others. Family members and friends, not to mention treating clinicians, can be key in helping people escape from abusive situations. With help and support, Jenny will be just fine.

Anyone who has worked in an emergency department has seen firsthand the truly horrific effects of intimate partner violence. Women (and, less often, men) who have been beaten and sometimes raped may be desperate enough to finally seek help. However, as we can attest to after having interviewed many women and men in this situation, short-term medical help is not enough, and victims are often too scared, intimidated, embarrassed, and ashamed to figure out how to get out of their current situation. If you are a victim of intimate partner violence, there is help, and often it can be found by simply trusting a primary care physician, nurse, social worker, or other mental health professional enough to share your story. There are many examples of women who have managed to escape abusive relationships and go on to lead amazing lives. One of them, Sara Hall, wrote a memoir about her experiences called *Drawn to the Rhythm*. She shares how, in the midst of an emotionally abusive marriage, she found the sport of rowing, and with the help of friends and family, discovered the strength to leave her husband and move on to a more fulfilling life as a mother, writer, consultant, and national champion rower.

• • •

In the next chapter, we'll discuss children who may be burgeoning almost or true psychopaths. Although it may seem reasonable to conclude that children who are brought up in difficult situations, such as witnessing intimate partner violence, are destined to develop psychopathic tendencies themselves, that's not necessarily true. As with adults, many genetic and environmental factors can play a role in how these children turn out. And the good news is that very often the earlier a problem is recognized in a child, the more effective appropriate interventions will be.

6

Recognizing Almost Psychopathic
Traits in Children

So far, we've been discussing almost psychopaths and psycho-paths as adults. What about when they were children? As our next life story shows, some of the same behaviors and attitudes that mark psychopathy can be found in adolescence and even childhood.

Sammy

Sammy was not really a "bad" child, at least not at first. But his parents did find him challenging, even in infancy. The term *terrible twos* seemed to have been invented for him; he was difficult to console when he was upset, and his crying was seemingly endless. When angry—and it didn't take much—he would thrash around, bang his head against the floor, and attempt to bite his parents. Two babysitters quit because they could not tolerate his rages. By age three, Sammy had calmed down a bit but was oppositional when asked to do things, at times still lashing out physically. Sammy's pediatrician explained that children are born with different temperaments, that they lie along a continuum, and that Sammy would likely grow out of the more problematic behaviors. And it was true; as he got older there were extended periods when Sammy seemed perfectly happy, content to sit with his parents and listen to a story. He was bright and asked good questions about the world around him. Sammy's dad was comforted by the thought that his own older brother had been like Sammy and had turned out okay. Perhaps the pediatrician was right.

Sammy's behavior did change. While he was never particularly cuddly, by age four he had learned that his chances of getting what he wanted increased if he crawled into his parents' laps or wrapped his arms around their necks or just looked at them and smiled. They were so happy to see some semblance of warmth and attachment that they quickly gave in to his requests. After all, shouldn't they reinforce that behavior? Sammy was a quick learner, but it wasn't clear who was training whom.

Preschool was no picnic for Sammy or for his classmates. Once he decided he wanted a toy, he would grab it, no matter who was playing with it. The child who resisted was met with a tug or a slap or, in some instances, a bite. The preschool teachers intervened and spoke to Sammy's parents. While he wasn't the only child who had ever exhibited this behavior, his was more extreme, and the teachers insisted that it had to stop. And it did stop, as other children learned to be wary of Sammy and give him whatever he wanted.

Kindergarten held more of the same. By the time Sammy was in first grade, the school became more concerned about his behavior, and a school psychologist was called in to assess him.

Sammy's parents were disturbed by the idea that their son was a problem student who needed psychological help, but the school assured them that they were just trying to address any emerging problems. Whether they would say it or not, Sammy's parents were hopeful that, finally, they could get some answers.

When he met with the psychologist, Sammy was pleasant and cooperative, playing the assessment games like an average six-year-old; however, he got bored easily and was distracted by other things in the office. The psychologist detected a fair amount of aggression in his storytelling and play with action figures. Testing revealed an above-average IQ but with indications of attention and concentration problems. Observing him in class, the psychologist noted that Sammy had trouble sitting still for extended periods of time and that his attention drifted to what was happening outside the window. At recess, she saw that the other children tended to avoid him, and when he did get involved in group play, arguments and fights followed. Still, Sammy had a few friends who got along with him and who would invite him to their houses.

Meeting with Sammy's parents, the psychologist described what she had found, assuring them that Sammy was quite bright but may have attention deficit hyperactivity disorder (ADHD) as well as some social learning skills deficits. She suggested that they talk with their pediatrician about medication to help him focus and recommended that they put him in a therapeutic playgroup. Sammy's parents were hesitant about the medication. The idea of giving a stimulant (the standard medication for ADHD) to a child who was already irritable and bouncing off the walls did not make sense to them. And when they spoke to their pediatrician, she supported them in taking a go-slow approach, suggesting that they try the playgroup first and see how it worked out.

The playgroup was helpful. Sammy learned new social skills and found that he would get rewarded for taking turns and letting others have their way, although he continued to find it hard to give in. His attention and hyperactivity did not improve, and he continued to have discipline problems at school because he pestered other children in class and spoke out of turn. But Sammy was smart, and his grades were more than good enough to get him promoted on schedule.

Soon enough, it was time to start high school. Just as the schoolwork was getting more demanding, adolescence had arrived for Sammy and his parents, with all the hormone surges and oppositional attitudes and behaviors that so often go with it. Sammy—Sam as he insisted they start calling him— began having more trouble with his studies, and the pediatrician reluctantly suggested that Sam try a stimulant medication to address his ADHD. It helped Sam focus a bit more in his classes and when he did his homework, but he hated taking it. And even if it helped, there were other distractions: girls, parties, and, eventually, experimenting with alcohol and drugs. At home, Sam was quiet and sullen; his behavior at school was similar, except when he was hanging out with his friends—often at detention because of disturbances they had caused in class.

In his sophomore year, Sam's parents took him to see another psychologist. Like the first, he noted Sam's intelligence, his ADHD, and his aggressive and hostile tendencies. Sam denied using alcohol or drugs and described his parents the way many adolescents do: "They're too strict, they won't let me do what I want, they don't like my music or my friends," and so on. He complained about this in family sessions with his parents, and they agreed to try to be "less controlling" and more open-minded if he would agree to behave better at home and in school. The psychologist recommended group therapy with other adolescents, but Sam refused to go, insisting that he wasn't a "nut case." Feeling powerless to force him to attend, Sam's parents went along with his refusal.

Junior year of high school started out as a mixed bag for the family. Sam shaped up his behavior a bit at home, his grades improved slightly, and his parents gave him more leeway. He took advantage of this and stayed out later at night with his friends, drinking, smoking pot, and engaging in generally obnoxious behavior in the town center, telling his parents that he was studying with classmates. His parents thought things were going reasonably well, although they still were worried about what the future would hold for their son. He had shown no indication of wanting to go to college or learn a trade, and he was halfway through his junior year.

Over the course of that year, Sam broke his curfew with increasing frequency, making up all sorts of excuses about why he was late. He was more argumentative at home and in school, almost coming to blows with a teacher on one occasion. His suspension from school for that incident was followed by another that was twice as long for throwing a cinderblock out a third-floor window onto a teacher's car. That was followed by a call from school that Sam had been caught selling his ADHD medication to other students, leaving Sam's parents feeling stunned and helpless. Things had been bad enough, but now the police were involved, and Sam had been expelled.

A family services evaluation ordered by the judge revealed that Sam had taken his ADHD medication only occasionally, saving up the pills to sell to students who used them to get high. Sam spent the money he made to buy other drugs at times, but mostly alcohol. Sam got probation from the court, was assigned a family services officer to keep an eye on him (including random urine drug screening), and was to begin studying for his general equivalency diploma. These were the most severe consequences he had ever experienced for his behavior, and for once, Sam seemed truly shaken. His parents set a strict curfew, denying him access to the car or taking away his cell phone for any infraction. Sam looked for a job, but little was available other than day labor. Frustrated with this, and having trouble remaining under the watchful eye of his parents, he eventually decided to join the army. No longer taking medication, and drug and alcohol free, Sam responded well to the discipline and structure of military service, where he found some others who were similar to him: bright young people who had had a rocky time in school and now were responding well to military life. Sam stuck with it and, like his uncle, did okay.

A Bad Seed?

The bad seed. You've heard the term, even if you haven't read the 1954 William March novel of that name or seen its stage or film adaptations. Ron assigns that book in his freshman seminar at Harvard College, and the students usually come back "creeped out" and often complain that they had trouble sleeping the night they read it.

The Bad Seed is the story of eight-year-old Rhoda Penmark, a bright, blond-haired, blue-eyed, overly polite and mature little girl who happens to be a killer. Skilled at manipulating others, completely focused on acquiring what she wants by any means, and a very effective liar, Rhoda, like her serial-killer grandmother she has never met, is a psychopath. Rooted in the prevailing psychoanalytic theory of the day, and long before the neuroscience and genetic studies of psychopathy, *The Bad Seed* explores the idea of psychopathy being transmitted genetically and appearing in children, even when there is no apparent environmental influence. Rhoda has a loving father, who happens to be living away on business, and a caring mother who is unaware that her own mother, Rhoda's grandmother, was the infamous Bessie Denker—a woman who killed people (including family members) for their money and insurance proceeds.

The Bad Seed is, of course, a novel and a stylized portrayal of psychopathy. Nonetheless it is an accurate rendition of psychopathy as described by the literature of the time, including Cleckley's *The Mask of Sanity*. Sammy's story is a bit more typical of problematic behaviors in children that may lead to concerns about psychopathy.

Too Young to Be a Psychopath?

There is some debate in the psychiatric community about whether it is appropriate to diagnose psychopathy in children and adolescents. Some developmental research supports the contention that the diagnosis should not be applied to youth.[57] Furthermore, experience tells us that some characteristics of psychopathy are an expected part of growing up. As the parent of any teenager will tell you, a less-than-generous consideration of the needs of others is a predictable stage that seems to begin immediately upon blowing out thirteen candles on a birthday cake. Not surprisingly, one study shows that egocentricity is typical at the adolescent stage of development. The impulsivity and poor planning of adolescents can be attributed to brain development; the nerve cells of the frontal lobes of the brain—the part of the brain largely responsible for impulse control and judgment—don't reach their maturity until the early twenties. Don't all teenagers get bored easily and crave stimulation? How about the grandiosity and invincibility of youth? You get the idea: behaviors that are normal in adolescence may resemble characteristics of psychopathy. Also, it is impossible or at least very difficult to accurately identify and assess interpersonal and behavioral deficits typical of psychopathy until the personality is more fully developed. (For example, a person's empathy may not be developed enough to assess in any meaningful way until perhaps adulthood.)

According to the American Psychiatric Association, antisocial personality disorder (the closest diagnosis the *DSM–IV–TR* has to psychopathy), like all personality disorders, cannot be officially diagnosed before the age of eighteen, although mental health experts can identify psychopathic traits before that time. The manual points out that personality disorders begin by late adolescence or early adulthood, and the signs of adult personality disorders—including antisocial, borderline, and narcissistic—can be detected even in childhood. Studies have shown that personality traits are present from the earliest days of infancy.[58] It follows, then, that it should be possible to measure certain characteristics of psychopathy—shallow affect, lack of empathy, and so on—before a person reaches adulthood. (It would seem odd that a person would suddenly appear to suffer from a severe personality disorder like psychopathy at age eighteen without having signs of problems in earlier years.) And if the characteristics of psychopathy are considered part of "normal development," it would seem likely that a higher percentage of teenagers would be diagnosed as psychopathic than adults, but the research does not bear this out; the rate of adolescent psychopathy in incarcerated juveniles is about the same or a little less than the rate of psychopathy in incarcerated adults.[59] Studies show that many children who display psychopathic traits—frequently called *callous unemotional traits* (not being concerned with the feelings of others, not feeling guilty)—will show those same traits as teens. While some of these teens seem simply to grow out of such traits, those with more significant callous unemotional traits are more likely to become psychopathic adults.

As part of the general increased interest in psychopathy, researchers have developed various tools to assess psychopathy in children and adolescents. These instruments essentially take the PCL–R and modify the questions and areas of assessment to an age-appropriate level; these are known as *downward developmental translations.* In the 1990s, experts including Robert Hare, the father of the checklist, developed the Antisocial Process Screening Device (APSD), an adaptation of the PCL–R meant to be sensitive to the developmental stage of children ages six to thirteen. This more age-appropriate APSD is completed by parents and teachers, but a self-report version also exists that has proven useful, particularly in situations where the child has spent time in an out-of-home placement. Another tool, the PCL–YV (Youth Version), also developed by Hare and others, is meant for use with older children, ages thirteen to eighteen. It is also a modified version of the PCL–R and again makes age-appropriate adjustments: for example, it emphasizes involvement with peers and schools. Both of these tools have been shown to have relatively high reliability. While the existence and use of these and other measuring tools does not definitively answer when the disorder can be accurately

A Second Glance

One indicator of psychopathic behavior is insufficient attention and response to emotional cues from other people. A 2010 study in Australia sought to show that this inattention begins early in life, as demonstrated by the failure of certain children to make eye contact with their parents.

Eye contact is one of the keys ways in which people pick up on the emotional state of others, and it plays an important role in the development of empathy and a social conscience. In this study, 92 boys between the ages of five and sixteen who had been referred to mental health centers in Australia were assessed for the presence of "callous, unemotional traits" (CU traits), which are considered potential indicators of a future diagnosis of psychopathy. The children were observed interacting with family members during a free-play time and on a separate occasion when they were asked to discuss a happy and a sad time they had shared with their parents. Both sets of interactions were recorded, and researchers analyzed the tapes for general social engagement styles and rates of eye contact between children and parents.

The results revealed that children with high CU trait measurements had less eye contact with parents. This fits with the idea that psychopathy is, in part, related to a failure to recognize distress in others, which leads to a failure to curtail aggressive behavior.[60]

diagnosed, the consensus among mental health professionals is that the disorder can be found in stages of development well before adulthood.

The Same as Adult Psychopathy or Different?

Some of the same considerations at play in the debate about the appropriateness of considering a child or youth to be an almost psychopath are relevant to the related question of whether psychopathy is expressed similarly in children as it is in adults. While a great deal of research shows that adult psychopathy comprises two broad factors—*affective-interpersonal attributes* (lack of empathy, glibness, superficial charm; factor 1) and *socially deviant behaviors* (poor behavioral controls, impulsivity, sensation seeking; factor 2)—it is not obvious that children would express psychopathy in the same way.

Research using the Antisocial Process Screening Device (APSD) and the Youth Version of the PCL has confirmed the idea that, in all, child and adolescent psychopathy resembles adult psychopathy and predicts psychopathy in adulthood. Nevertheless, a recent study in California investigating the role of genetic and environmental factors in childhood psychopathy yielded slightly different results. Participants in the study were recruited from Los Angeles County and were part of the Southern California Twin Project. The total sample consisted of 605 sets of nine- and ten-year-old twins and triplets and their primary caregivers, representing an ethnically and socioeconomically diverse population. The children and their caregivers were invited for a full day of assessments. The caregivers were given a self-report questionnaire and also interviewed about the childrens' behavior at home and in school.

Psychopathy was measured using the Child Psychopathy Scale, a version of the PCL–R modified for use with children and adolescents. The study results provided support for both genetic and unique environmental influences on psychopathy in children and adolescents.[61] As with adults, both nature and nurture seem to play a role in the expression of almost psychopathy and true psychopathy in children and adolescents.

The results of this twins study also showed that, as with adult psychopathy, two factors account for child and adolescent psychopathy. Interestingly, however, the two factors in children and adolescents differ slightly from the descriptions of factors found in adult psychopathy. The differences, though, are not profound (in fact, other studies with children and adolescents have shown little if any distinction), and any differences may be traced to a number of factors (for instance, the instruments used in diagnosing psychopathy, the PCL–R and Child Psychopathy Scale, are not identical). And the fact that there *are* differences can be seen as encouraging. It perhaps suggests that mental health professionals may find more success treating children and adolescents with existing methods than they have had to date with adult psychopaths. It even may encourage the development of new treatments aimed specifically at this age group. Ultimately, researchers hope that the studies on the psychopathic personality in children and adolescents will help them to develop more effective intervention programs and to identify those who would most benefit from such treatments. As the authors of the twins research study noted of their own work, "However, these results in no way imply that children are not capable of change or that they are impervious to intervention and prevention methods."[62]

It's Not All about Crime

What about children whose behaviors may not meet the full definition of psychopathy? Are there almost psychopaths among children and adolescents? To answer this question, we might consider the self-servingly callous or deceitful behavior that might appear in situations that kids and adolescents most often encounter. Behavior at school (like the mean girls we discussed in chapter 4) might be a good indicator. And why do students plagiarize papers and copy answers on tests? The answer has long been assumed to be as simple as it is obvious—kids who struggle academically cheat so they can "keep up" with their peers and their parents' expectations. New research, though, shows that personality, not learning difficulties, may be a much more accurate predictor of who will cheat. It turns out that students who cheat in high school and college may well be almost psychopaths who plagiarize and crib because they feel entitled and are readily able to disregard conventional morality that holds back others from doing the same.

Three studies from the University of British Columbia found that college students who admitted cheating in high school ranked high on personality tests of the so-called Dark Triad: psychopathy, Machiavellianism (manipulativeness, cynicism, amorality), and narcissism (arrogance and self-centeredness). Of these three, psychopathy was the most clearly associated with cheating.[63]

In the first study, about 250 college students (whose anonymity was protected) were asked if, during high school, they had handed in work that was not their own or had cheated on tests. These same students (also anonymously) filled out personality tests that measured traits, including those of the Dark

Triad, as well as traits of extroversion, agreeableness, conscientiousness, stability, and openness. The result of this study was clear: the higher students ranked on the psychopathy scale, the more likely they had engaged in academic dishonesty.

A second study looked at actual, not self-reported, cheating by analyzing two papers written by students: one on a research topic, another on a personal experience. The students took the same personality tests and *were told* that their submissions would be scanned by an online service that compares the submissions to papers included in a database. While it might seem that being warned that their work was going to be carefully analyzed by a software program designed to detect cheating would eliminate all traces of plagiarism, that was not the case. Of the 114 participants, 16 were found to have plagiarized on at least one essay. Once again, the most significant association with cheating was a high score on the psychopathy scale.

The third study had a different twist. Instead of looking at whether students cheat, the purpose was to see why they cheat. A group of 223 college students took personality tests in which they were asked to rate themselves on a self-report cheating scale that included items such as "I needed to get (or keep) a scholarship" or "I'm not concerned about punishment if caught." The data revealed a number of students who thought that cheating was an acceptable means for attaining their goals, were not deterred by potential punishments, and were not morally inhibited. A higher score on the psychopathy scale was strongly linked to all three of these factors.

The desire to do well academically is shared by many high school and college students. It's the fuel for all-night study sessions and weekends spent in the library and not the frat house. The difference with students who are almost psycho-paths, though, is that they feel entitled to get good grades and appear not to care that cheating is wrong. As with adults who are almost psychopaths, these adolescents (and young adults) are most keenly interested in what is best for them, with little or no regard to the rules that apply to the situation.

In extreme cases, academic dishonesty can go well beyond cheating on a few tests or handing in a paper purchased on the Internet. In fact, in the 1988 edition of his seminal work *The Mask of Sanity*, Cleckley discusses several case histories of almost psychopaths (what he calls "incomplete manifestations or suggestions of the disorder"), one of whom had cheated and plagiarized his way through a variety of renowned institutions of higher learning. In 2010, the Ivy League had its own exam-ple of such behavior when Harvard University discovered that it had admitted a student based on a fictitious academic record and personal history.

When Adam Wheeler applied to Harvard as a transfer stu-dent, he indicated that he had graduated from Phillips Academy, an elite prep school in Massachusetts, and had attended the Massachusetts Institute of Technology. He submitted four letters of recommendation from MIT professors, essays about his time at MIT, and documents showing that he had received a perfect SAT score of 1,600. In reality, he had graduated from a public high school in Delaware, had attended Bowdoin College for two years before being suspended for academic dishonesty, and received SAT scores of 1,160 and 1,220 the two times he took the test in 2004. Those letters of recommendation from MIT professors? The letters actually were in the names of professors from Bowdoin, although all asserted that they had not written any recommendation for Wheeler. Wheeler's deception was not limited to falsifying papers. As part of the transfer application process, Wheeler had to interview with a Harvard alumnus. At the interview held at Bowdoin, the interviewer wondered what an MIT student was doing in Maine. Wheeler had a ready answer: he had finished his work at MIT for the semester and had moved to Bowdoin to work for a professor.

During the two years he was at Harvard, Wheeler continued his conning ways, winning prestigious academic competitions and research grants with plagiarized work. His undoing? Not content to graduate with a degree from Harvard, Wheeler went a step too far. In 2009, he applied for the Rhodes and Fulbright scholarships, and one of the professors reviewing the applications saw similarities between a paper Wheeler submitted and the work of another Harvard professor. This professor reported his suspicions to school authorities, and soon the game was up. A thorough review of Wheeler's application revealed that he had used a fake transcript (showing a straight A student, which he was not), plagiarized the paper he submitted, and otherwise lied on his application—he had not co-authored any of the books, given any of the lectures, or taught any of the courses he listed. Wheeler was dismissed from Harvard.

In 2010, he was indicted in Massachusetts on charges including identity theft and larceny ("stealing" the grants, scholarships, and aid he received from Harvard). He eventually pleaded guilty to twenty misdemeanor and felony counts and was sentenced to ten years of probation, ordered to pay restitution of over $40,000, and barred from profiting from his case by writing a book or selling his story. (In late 2011, there were calls to revoke Wheeler's probation and have him serve out his sentence: he had reportedly violated the terms of his probation by listing Harvard University on his résumé.)

Children and adolescents who display almost psychopathic traits also engage in other nonviolent antisocial behaviors aside from cheating in school. Turning back to our example of Sammy, we see a particular and troubling habit that is frequently associated with adolescents with psychopathic tendencies: heavy use of alcohol. By the time he was in high school, Sam was drinking regularly, even going so far as to sell his ADHD medication for money to buy alcohol. A 2011 study suggested a link between certain features of psychopathy—and the closely related antisocial personality disorder—and heavy drinking in college students. In this investigation, 159 undergraduates at a private university (85 male and 74 female) completed a self-report assessment of alcohol use and the frequency and consequences of heavy episodic drinking, as well as a personality test. The study found that the presence of psychopathy, independent of any antisocial personality disorder, was useful in predicting heavy episodic drinking and the difficulties resulting from it.[64] So, while Sam may not have been a full-blown clinical psychopath, he certainly shared at least one behavior often associated with young psychopaths—frequent and heavy drinking. Thankfully, as we saw, his parents were committed to getting him the help he needed and he ultimately found his way to a more stable life.

A Different Outcome?

It's important to keep in mind, particularly if you are dealing with someone like Sammy in your life, that none of the research has shown that children or adolescents with almost psychopathic traits will invariably stay that way. As with many facets of the developing personality, the disorder is not necessarily permanent, or at least has not been proved to be so. Growing up is tough work, and part of that work involves developing a more or less objective view of oneself and the world as a whole. Yet those views are not always accurate and may even include attitudes and lead to behaviors that might be considered psychopathic. Adults, as well as adolescents, may exhibit behaviors and attitudes that arise from cognitive distortions—impressions and interpretations of the self and the world inconsistent with how others would view the same events. Closing the gap between those views and reality is an important part of growing up. Not everyone is succeeds in closing that gap, but most do.

One consideration with children who exhibit early signs of psychopathy is whether they can be taught empathy. Most researchers think this is unlikely. As suggested in a 2011 study conducted in France and the United States, a better approach to addressing the antisocial behavior of adolescents—even those with psychopathic traits—may be to focus on their self-serving cognitive distortions through treatment, such as cognitive behavioral therapy.[65] It may also be helpful to try to modify their behavior gradually by demonstrating that it is in their self-interest to conform to society's rules, whether they care about those rules or not. In other words, try to shape their behavior by showing them that violating rules or running roughshod over the feelings of others is maladaptive and is *less* likely to help them reach their goals. Reinforcing these ideas, as well as normalizing the behavior that usually comes with age and development, may help many people like Sammy get back on the path to normal and productive adult lives.

Finding the optimal balance of rewards and punishment that will help modify a child's behavior can be tricky under any circumstances, and even more so when elements suggestive of psychopathic behavior are present. As with adults, children with psychopathic traits do not appear to learn well from punishment. Findings from an Australian study of boys ages four to eight who had a history of conduct issues suggest that rewards are more effective than punishments with children who have callous unemotional traits. The children in the study did not respond to common strategies like time-outs (which is expected in children who have almost psychopathic tendencies, since one trait is that they are relatively insensitive to punishment). They did, however, react positively when their parents praised them for good behavior. A better strategy than alternating rewards and punishment may be to alternate rewards and withholding of rewards: the penalty is an absence of reward, rather than the imposition of a task, spanking, or time-out.

For most parents, their own happiness is largely influenced by the happiness of their children. Perhaps you have heard the phrase "You are only as happy as your least happy child," or used it yourself. As it did for Sammy's parents, the inability to console and comfort one's child when he or she is sick or hurt can cause great sadness and frustration. Sammy's parents picked up that he was experiencing problems, even though they had no idea what those were early on. They did the right thing by consulting their pediatrician. Unfortunately, the pediatrician took an approach that, while supportive, did not help Sammy or his parents address the problem.

"Watch and wait" is not always a helpful strategy when a family encounters problems like this, as the relationship between the parents and their child—not to mention the child's chances for other normal relationships—can be seriously and negatively affected by these difficulties. This is a situation in which the parents and the child need maximum support from family and friends, as well as professionals. That professional support is best delivered through a team approach that can include a child psychiatrist, psychologist, social worker, educational consultant, and perhaps an occupational therapist, depending on what is found through a thorough assessment. Sammy needed an educational assessment early on and did seem to have benefited from a therapeutic playgroup. Family therapy, with a professional watching the family interact and suggesting ways to improve their interactions and communication, would also have helped. Medication might have been appropriate for this child early on. And Sammy's parents would have benefited from an evaluation to determine if they had developed anxiety or depression prior to, or in response to, the struggles with Sammy. Failure to treat those could have a negative effect on Sammy and his hopes of improvement.

The challenge for Sammy's parents was to set firm and reasonable limits on his out-of-control behavior—throughout his childhood and adolescence—while still remaining loving and supportive. At some point, parents of children who do not show signs of improvement may need to step back from the situation and let the child take responsibility for the consequences of his or her behavior, until it changes. Regardless of how the situation plays out, they will likely need professional help, as well as a great deal of support from family and friends.

■ ❖ ■

7

Working with an Almost Psychopath

The workplace is a prime location for encountering high-functioning almost psychopaths. Some of these, like Greta in our next example, can succeed for years, deceiving and taking advantage of those around them.

Greta

Greta was a star. Since early childhood, she rarely failed at anything. Extremely bright, talented in multiple fields, athletic, and attractive, she was always the center of attention growing up. And when she wasn't, she did whatever was necessary to change that. When she was young, that could include manipulating adults, telling tales about other children, and sometimes outright lying. Everyone in the community knew little Greta—it was hard to ignore such a talent—but very few could say that they liked her. While parents initially encouraged their children to become friends with this smart, athletic child, they generally changed their minds when their kids came home in tears after some belittling remark or other from Greta and begged to not have to play with her again.

Some children grow up but really don't change. Greta was one of those. She was enthusiastically courted by and then admitted to a top college where she charmed the professors and alienated her classmates. What started out as close friendships (primarily with people whom she thought could be of use to her) quickly dissolved after disputes over "borrowed" items of clothing, snide comments, and stolen boyfriends.

In graduate school, where she earned both an advanced science degree and an MBA, it was more of the same. At one point in her science graduate school career, the laboratory notebook of one of her classmates (who happened to be Greta's top competitor for academic honors) went missing. As the classmate became increasingly worried that she would have to repeat the experiments for her thesis, Greta joined in offering condolences and words of support. Nevertheless, suspicion turned to her. One classmate quietly warned Greta that she was a suspect; not long after, the notebook was found on a shelf in the supply room.

In business school, Greta again wowed the professors. She was articulate and persuasive, both when she responded to questions in class and when she presented group projects— which she invariably insisted on doing. Greta's expert social skills prevented her from claiming sole responsibility for all of the group's ideas, but she definitely represented that she was involved in the creation of all the ideas presented, even those that had not been hers or that she had initially opposed. Her classmates were never sure whether this was a matter of good business sense—challenging an idea, allowing oneself to be

WORKING WITH AN ALMOST PSYCHOPATH ❖

persuaded, and then advocating for it once convinced—or
something else. At graduation, she received a special award
for leadership in the classroom. Classmates who knew her well
were dismayed, some of them suggesting that she should have
received a psychopath award.

After business school, Greta got a job with a top consulting
firm, where she put both her science and business skills to good
use. Consistent with her past behavior, she "managed up" very
well—winning over the senior partners of the firm, or at least
the males, with her charm and intelligence. She was brought
along to new client meetings, where she was often helpful in
selling her firm's services. But while she could do no wrong in
the eyes of many of the partners, others were less convinced. As
friendly as she was with the male partners, she was far more
distant from the female partners, as if she viewed them as com-
petitors. She treated support staff terribly, making unreasonable
demands and pointing out the differences in their educational
backgrounds when anyone questioned her requests. She got
along a bit better with peers, at least until she felt the need to
"throw them under the bus." The word at the water cooler was
that you had better watch out for that bus if you were in direct
competition with Greta for promotion or attention, or if she
had made an error and needed to shift blame to someone else.

Clients were often enamored of Greta when she first started
to work with them. But, as with her peers, the honeymoon
didn't last long. On one trip to visit a client, she complained
about the food in the company cafeteria and the midrange
hotel they arranged, insisting that they send out for meals and
move her to a more expensive hotel. All of this, of course, went
on the client's bill. She was abrupt with the client's support

staff, just as she was at her own firm, although her disregard for them did not stop her from asking them to do personal favors for her. When Stephan, the chief financial officer of the client company, saw the invoices from Greta's consulting firm and all the additional charges from Greta's demands, he started inquiring about how the project was going. Once he heard about her interactions with company staff, he called Maria, the managing partner at Greta's firm, and gave her an ultimatum: if you ever send Greta back here again, we'll find new consultants.

By this point, Maria was not surprised; this was just one in a series of complaints she had received about Greta over several months. At first, Maria discounted the criticisms as typical workplace grumbling, but the number and consistency of the complaints made it clear that Greta was a real problem. Maria had planned to discuss these issues during Greta's performance review the next month but now felt she could not wait.

When Greta was summoned to Maria's office, she arrived a few minutes late, as was her habit, and Maria showed her annoyance when Greta finally breezed in. Greta smiled and apologized, saying that she had been on the phone with Stephan to talk about the next steps in the project. Maria was astounded; she knew Greta was lying because she had just hung up the phone with Stephan, after promising him that he would never have to see or work with Greta again. Maria decided to take the bold approach and confront Greta with her obvious untruth, wanting to see her reaction. Greta didn't miss a beat, apologizing for the confusion and explaining that she meant to say Pete, a client with whom she had just started to work and still had a good relationship. Maria wasn't sure what to believe now. But if Greta is lying, she thought to herself, she sure is good.

Maria asked Greta if she knew why she had asked her to come in for the meeting. Looking at her directly—almost through her—and with her trademark smile, Greta said she knew it was time for her performance review, and she assumed that Maria was calling her in to give her a raise and a promotion because of the quality work she had done for Stephan's firm and others. "No, not quite," Maria answered. "I just have to tell you, that, while your technical skills are excellent, your people skills are so poor that no one—colleagues or clients—wants to work with you." She ran through a list of complaints and problems, ending with Stephan's threat to fire the firm if Greta were sent back. Greta's smile never wavered. When Maria finished, she asked Greta if she had anything to say. Greta responded by saying that she appreciated the feedback and looked forward to her raise and promotion. Then she stood up, gave Maria one more big smile, and left the office.

Completely unnerved by Greta's reaction, Maria found the phone number for the psychiatrist whom the firm had on retainer for consulting about problem employees. It was no surprise (or disappointment) to Maria when Greta left the firm shortly thereafter, when a headhunter sought her out for a competing consulting firm. Nor was she surprised when she learned of Greta's lawsuit against the firm, claiming that she had had to quit because of the hostile work environment, discrimination, and harassment of all types.

Female Psychopaths

While most of the research involving psychopathy has focused on men, particularly men who are incarcerated, the relatively few studies on women and psychopathy leave little doubt that there are female psychopaths and female almost psychopaths. In fact, Cleckley included female examples in later editions of *The Mask of Sanity*. What is not as clear is the *prevalence* of psychopathy and almost psychopathy in the female population as compared to the male population. Some studies seem to indicate that the overall rate of psychopathy among incarcerated women is similar to the overall rate among incarcerated men,[66] although other studies have indicated a much lower rate among incarcerated women.[67]

Other research indicates that psychopathy in females may develop on a different trajectory than in males. For example, antisocial adolescent boys who have a history of early-onset conduct problems have both higher levels of callous unemotional traits than their antisocial peers with no history of early-onset conduct problems and are more likely to be labeled psychopaths as adults. This pattern does not hold true for adolescent girls for the simple reason that childhood-onset conduct problems are rarely found in young girls. Interestingly, though, some girls do begin to show conduct problems in adolescence that are similar to those experienced by boys with early-onset conduct problems (impulse-control issues and elevated levels of callous unemotional personality traits). Once they reach adulthood, those same girls are more likely to be classified as psychopaths than their peers.[68] And the *types* of aggressive behavior that female psychopaths engage in may differ somewhat from the aggressive actions of males: females are less likely than males to use overt forms of aggression (punching, kicking) and more likely to rely on covert forms of aggression related to their social groups (gossiping, ostracism—which is sometimes called *relational aggression*).

Almost Psychopaths in the Workplace

Swiss psychiatrist Adolf Guggenbühl-Craig, author of *The Emptied Soul: On the Nature of the Psychopath* (1980), believes that there are many psychopaths who hold upstanding positions in society, including businesspeople. He refers to them as *compensated psychopaths*. We call them almost psychopaths or subclinical psychopaths. It makes sense that people who are almost psychopaths can be found in the business world; psychopaths are attracted to power and money the way sharks are attracted to chum. Many psychopaths thrive on fast-moving situations where the outcome is what matters. And while robbing banks might make sense to psychopaths who score high on the "socially deviant lifestyle" elements of the PCL–R, those whose psychopathic traits are more heavily weighted in the direction of narcissism and Machiavellianism would more likely be attracted to a corporate setting where, in many cases, they can be rewarded for their manipulative and ruthless ways.

The developer of the PCL–R himself, Robert Hare, has observed that in addition to studying psychopaths in prison, he should have spent time at the Stock Exchange as well.[69] His point was that there is no shortage of psychopathic behavior in the business world, no end to the charming, manipulative, credit-stealing, colleague-blaming conduct that defines psychopathy. These almost psychopathic and truly psychopathic managers and executives can create havoc on a somewhat limited level by, say, creating dissension in a sales department, but also on a much larger scale, where an instinct toward self-centered manipulation and lack of integrity can bring down an entire corporation, causing financial and emotional damage to thousands or tens of thousands (think Enron).

In 2005, two psychologists at the University of Surrey, England, published their research comparing the personality profiles of high-level British executives ("senior business managers") with randomly selected psychiatric patients and criminal psychiatric patients at Broadmoor Special Hospital, a high-security hospital in the United Kingdom and home to some of Britain's most notorious criminals.[70] The psychologists administered the Minnesota Multiphasic Personality Inventory Scales for DSM–III Personality Disorders (MMPI–PD), a true/false self-report inventory in which the respondent is asked to consider statements reflecting eleven different personality disorders: histrionic, narcissistic, antisocial, borderline, dependent, obsessive-compulsive, passive-aggressive, paranoid, schizotypal, schizoid, and avoidant.

The psychologists were particularly interested in measuring these traits in senior business managers because of previous work suggesting some psychopaths operate in mainstream society and because of the links made between elements of these almost psychopaths and character traits associated with success in business. Noting that the evidence of almost psychopaths is growing (the psychologists in this study used the term *successful psychopaths*), they also highlighted research indicating that the emotion factor is higher than the deviant lifestyle/antisocial factor in successful psychopaths. In other words, almost (successful) psychopaths who flourish in the business world are proficient manipulators and influencers who are less prone to overt rule and law breaking than true psychopaths. More specifically, almost psychopaths seem to have particular proficiency for seeking out and developing relationships with people of high authority and influencing them.

For this study, the psychologists contacted senior business managers and chief executive officers of British industry, informing them of the purpose of the study and inviting them to participate. Of the fifty-one who initially agreed to take part, only thirty-nine actually did. The executive sample was 100 percent male, and the average length of employment was over eight years in the current organization. These participants were either seen at their offices and interviewed to obtain background information and then invited to complete the MMPI–PD, or were contacted by letter and given the MMPI–PD and a demographic sheet and asked to return them to the researchers. Data for the psychiatric sample was obtained from a previous research sample of 475 randomly selected patients. For the sample of criminal psychiatric patients, 1,085 current and former patients at Broadmoor Special Hospital were selected. These current or former patients all had the classification of psychopathic disorder or mental illness. No women were selected for this sample to create a more direct comparison with the sample of exclusively male executives. Data for the Broadmoor patients was gathered from an existing database at the hospital.

For our purposes, the most interesting results of the study came from the comparison of the senior business executives to the offenders at Broadmoor. The study showed that three out of the eleven personality disorders were more common in the senior business managers than in the criminal psychiatric patients. These were histrionic personality disorder (superficial charm, insincerity, manipulation), narcissistic personality disorder (grandiosity, lack of empathy), and obsessive-compulsive personality disorder (perfectionism, excessive devotion to work,

rigidity, dictatorial tendencies) scales. Of the other eight personality disorders tested for (antisocial, borderline, dependent,
passive-aggressive, paranoid, schizotypal, schizoid, and avoidant), the criminal psychiatric patients outscored the senior business managers. Not surprisingly, the senior business managers
were less likely to express physical aggression, impulsivity, and
antisocial and paranoid tendencies.[71]

These findings make sense in relation to what we know
about true psychopaths. While in some cases the successful
executive may be a full-blown psychopath, it would probably be
difficult for such a person to last very long in a controlled environment. "Breaking the rules" might be an effective short-term
strategy in a business setting, but a true psychopath would find
it difficult to control his or her rule breaking (and backstabbing
and egocentricity and insincerity and . . .) well enough to stay
employed for long in any kind of structured organization. This
isn't to say that it's impossible. These are for-profit organizations we're talking about—their mission is to generate a profit
for shareholders, and if someone contributes significantly to that
goal, whether as an employee or the CEO, a board of directors
might be willing to overlook almost anything, at least until the
costs begin to outweigh the benefits. It is a common human failing that our capacity for objectivity can be limited when it comes
to someone who is benefiting us or with whom we are close.

Those who have only *some* of the characteristic traits of a
psychopath and are only almost psychopaths (like those executives in the British study who didn't show a strong tendency to
social deviance and law breaking) may have just what it takes
to charm their way into jobs and may have the conniving,
ruthless, and narcissistic personas necessary to work their way

to the top—even if it means stepping on others to get there. These high-performing executives are not likely to be serial killers or rapists; instead, the psychopathic behaviors that fuel their rise in the organization are more benign, and the colleagues and subordinates who fall prey to them are likely to think of them as backstabbers or bullies, while others may admire them for having what it takes to succeed in a dog-eat-dog world.

Workplace Bullies

Like schoolyard bullying, workplace bullying is a pattern of behavior where a person (or group of persons) engages in persistent aggressive behavior against a subordinate or co-worker. The key features of bullying (as opposed to isolated instances of bad behavior) are that it occurs regularly, goes on for some time, escalates over time, and is based on a "power disparity" where the target lacks the power or means to defend against the intimidation. As with other types of harassment, its goal is often to send a message to the victim that he or she does not belong there and that continuation in the workplace is dependent upon giving in to the demands and control of the bully/harasser.

Even if you've been bullied or seen bullying behavior at work, you may not realize how widespread the problem is. Two 2010 surveys (one with 4,210 respondents and the other with 2,092 respondents, both representative of all adults in the country at the time) revealed that 9 percent of US employees were currently being bullied, 26 percent had been bullied in the past, and 15 percent had seen or were aware of workplace bullying.[72] The vast majority of bullies (72 percent, according to the same 2010 survey) "outrank" their victims, and the majority of workplace bullies are men (62 percent, according to the survey).

Of course, not all bullies are almost psychopaths or true psychopaths. Some simply may have concluded that being strong or mean is what it takes for them to "win" at work. And many have come to this attitude honestly—having learned it by word and example from one or both parents, or even from those who trained them or from the media. Perhaps these workplace bullies act differently with their families or in the neighborhood, showing compassion after five and on the weekends. Not so with almost psychopaths or true psychopaths. They are unlikely to change their stripes, as it were, when they leave the site or office—either because they can't or they see no reason to do so unless it serves their interests in an obvious and immediate way. No matter how charming they seem in first

Medical Bullies?

For years, medicine had a tradition of irascible, emotionally—and sometimes physically—abusive attending physicians teaching medical students and residents. Anyone who has watched the television show *House* has seen prime examples of such behavior. As amusing and intriguing as it may be on television, the behavior is harmful to the trainees and ultimately to patient care. Whether it is justified as a form of indoctrination into the rigors of medicine or "tough love" or recognized as outright abuse, that behavior was too often transmitted from generation to generation as the residents exposed to it went on to become attending physicians and treat their trainees the same way. The American Medical Association, state medical boards, and the agencies responsible for medical education have now taken a strong stand against such behavior, considering it "disruptive" and potentially damaging to both patient care and education, and a potential basis for discipline of those who engage in it.

encounters, over time they will show themselves to be cold-hearted and manipulative, whether you run into them at a church social or the grocery store. Being an almost psychopath isn't just a workplace strategy—it's a way of life. And a way of misery for those whose lives they touch.

One Key to Their Success

As we have said, part of what distinguishes an almost psychopath from a true psychopath has to do with how well the person functions in society. For example, is he or she able to avoid committing serious social and legal transgressions that lead to prison and isolation? Instead, is he or she able to form a long-term intimate relationship, hold a job, and perhaps even achieve a great deal of success as a politician, businessman, physician, or lawyer? An important question is *how* almost psychopaths are able to live different lives than more criminally minded and disruptive psychopaths. Certainly, one possible explanation is that almost psychopaths simply have a brain wired for less pronounced psychopathic tendencies. In other words, they are wired more like the rest of us, with at least some capacity for empathy, insight, and remorse. But what about those "almosts" who are closer to true psychopaths? In a professional or business setting, these might be the almost psychopaths who achieve the greatest level of success. What is it that keeps them from straying into true psychopath territory? Researchers have long been interested in finding a clearer answer to this intriguing and important question.

First, though, these researchers had to deal with a practical issue that has long proved problematic in the study of almost psychopaths: how do you recruit them to participate in a study in the first place? By definition, these almost psychopaths are not in the criminal justice system and have not come to the attention of forensic psychiatrists or psychologists. Instead of being in prison or a mandated treatment program, they are in corporate board meetings, courtrooms, and medical offices.

In the 1970s, a researcher tried to recruit participants through advertisements seeking "charming, aggressive, carefree people who are impulsively irresponsible but are good at handling people and looking after number one" (a similar approach was used in a 1985 study). These ads did bring in participants, but given that many of the respondents in both studies had arrest records and low socioeconomic status, it is not clear that the goal of attracting successful psychopaths was met.

In a 2010 study entitled "The Search for the Successful Psychopath," researchers took a different tack; instead of trying to recruit almost psychopaths and directly assess them, they decided to have people in the business, legal, and medical fields do it for them. The researchers surveyed hundreds of members of the American Psychological Association's psychology and law division, criminal attorneys, and professors of clinical psychology about whether they had ever personally known someone who was successful in his or her field and who they believed would also have matched Hare's description of a psychopath—a person who is lacking in empathy and is charming, manipulative, and merciless.[73] Of the 118 APA members, 31 attorneys, and 58 psychology professors who replied, the majority (81, 25, and 41, respectively) said they had known a successful (almost) psychopath. The examples cited by the respondents were mostly male and included a range of students, colleagues, and friends whom the respondents had known for an average of over ten years. The respondents described these people's backgrounds in some detail ("dean of a major university," "mayor for three years," "managerial position in government organization") as well as their psychopathic tendencies ("utter absence of empathy," "chronic deceitfulness"). It turns out that at least one essential difference between the two groups—successful (almost) and true psychopaths—appears to be *conscientiousness.* The successful (almost) psychopaths described by the respondents rated high on competence, order, and self-discipline, whereas true psychopaths are usually rated high in irresponsibility, impulsivity, and negligence. Of course, the results of any study relying on retrospective assessments by colleagues and friends, and not on analysis through a controlled trial, are subject to a certain amount of skepticism. After all, there is no way to be certain that the colleagues knew the individuals they labeled as successful psychopaths well enough to make an informed evaluation. On the other hand, perhaps they knew them *too* well and substituted bias or personal enmity for objective judgment. Nevertheless, the fact that a fairly wide-ranging sample of people from different professions seemed to agree that the successful psychopaths they knew (or had known) displayed high levels of competence, self-discipline, and achievement striving (among other conscientiousness traits) is powerful evidence that successful almost psychopaths succeed at least in part because they can exert self-control in a way that true psychopaths apparently cannot.

Along these lines, Guggenbühl-Craig believes that compensated almost psychopaths are morally rigid, with a rule-following personality and a fierce determination to carry out perceived "duties." So almost psychopaths might not be any more empathetic than their more psychopathic cousins, but they do seem to be somewhat better at conforming to at least some of the rules of the game. He cites Adolph Eichmann, the architect of the Nazis' "final solution" during the Holocaust, as an example of a compensated psychopath. Morally rigid and devoted to the Nazi cause, Eichmann wrote that he went to sleep feeling guilty that he had failed his "duty" when the time came that he did not have enough personnel and materials to carry out his mass murders.

Smoking Them Out

While almost psychopaths may rise to positions of authority and responsibility in some companies and be considered assets, it is also true that they will be more likely to engage in bullying behaviors that could have serious repercussions (such as lawsuits by victims of workplace intimidation) and that their rule-breaking mentality and ruthlessness could lead them to commit fraud or land their employer in trouble with the government. Smart businesses will want to know which, if any, of their people are psychopaths or almost psychopaths. The trick is to identify almost psychopaths in a world where certain hallmarks of psychopathy—say, narcissism and grandiosity—are commonplace and, to some degree, desirable.

Existing tests for psychopathy, most notably the PCL–R, can be impractical to implement in a corporate setting, requiring both a one-on-one interview by a trained mental health expert and a thorough review of historical records (school, discipline, criminal, and so on). Not only is this a time-consuming process, but it is also unlikely that a human resources department would have access to the types of historical information required for an accurate assessment. (How many companies ask for an applicant's elementary school discipline records?) Another difficulty with PCL–R assessment, as well as the self-report psychopathy instruments, is that managers and executives could find it so highly personal and intrusive that they would resist participation. After all, these aren't convicted felons who are under the control of courts or prisons, and who can be ordered to speak with a psychiatrist.

To address these and other difficulties, Hare and industrial psychologist Paul Babiak are developing an instrument that screens for psychopathic tendencies in managers and executives and that does not require a one-on-one interview. The B-Scan (business scan) is a questionnaire designed to assess the types of behaviors and attitudes expressed by a person in various organizational situations. The test assesses four major areas—personal style, emotional style, organizational effectiveness, and social responsibility—by looking at various subcategories, such as "insincere," "untrustworthy," "arrogant," "blaming," "impatient," "erratic," and "bullying." There is both a self-report version (where the manager or executive answers the questions) and a supervisor version (given to current and former supervisors). Both versions can be done on paper or online, and take about fifteen minutes to complete.

How companies might use the scores in hiring and promotion decisions will vary. Different companies probably will have different views as to what level of psychopathic tendencies would be beneficial and how much the company culture can tolerate. And this analysis might vary from department to department. A certain amount of risk-taking nature might be helpful in sales but decidedly less advantageous in accounting. Undoubtedly, some managers and executives will have scores indicative of true psychopathy, and it might make sense to ease them out before they create (more) havoc.

What to Do?

So what do you do if you think the person in the next cubicle might be an almost psychopath? In other words, how best to handle your personal "Greta"? Using a staged approach to these situations makes sense, starting with the decision that you can, and should, stand up for yourself. If it's possible to do so without risk to yourself and your position, talk to your Greta and confront her, gently but directly, about her behavior. Tread cautiously if Greta is your supervisor. Perhaps if somewhere along the line someone had set some limits on the Greta we discussed earlier and she experienced some consequences for her behavior, she would have gotten the message. But for whatever reason, some pretty bright and normally assertive people, like her business school classmates, let her slide.

If you do decide to raise the issue with the person, go into the conversation with a clear idea of your concern and what needs to be changed. As you state your case, be positive and assertive in framing the issue. Avoid words that suggest you are unjustified in bringing it up and that amount to an apology, such as "Maybe I'm just being too sensitive, but . . ." Such language puts you one-down in addressing a conflict, and for an almost psychopath that show of weakness can be like blood in the water to a shark. Be clear, be firm, but be open to hearing what comes next. Remember, you are trying to solve a problem, not crush the person with whom you have a conflict. At the same time, you must keep in mind that this person may be trying to crush you.

Once you have stated your concerns, listen closely for the response. Is there immediate and outright denial? Is the response an attempt to explain away your concern and shift blame to others, including you? Or is there a willingness and ability to consider your concerns, even if he or she does not fully agree? The first type of response—outright denial—suggests that the person you are confronting realizes, at least at some level, that you are right and the person knows that his or her position is weak. Unless the individual can change this posture, the prognosis is not good for resolving the problem, unless you possess some exceptional conflict-resolution skills. The second type of response—blaming others—may indicate that you are dealing with someone with some psychopathic traits. The third response—a willingness to consider your concerns—is more positive, however, and suggests that this is a conflict that can be resolved and perhaps provide the basis for a stronger relationship.

Why don't we act sooner when we get into these situations? First, there is our usual reluctance to think poorly of others ("Is she really that bad? Maybe it won't happen again"). And then there is our resistance to the idea that someone who is like us is actually a bad person. ("C'mon. Nobody that well educated and that lovely could be so horrible.") And let's not forget about fear. That includes the fear that you are wrong and will get Greta in trouble for no reason, the fear of retribution that Greta has instilled in you if you are right, and the fear that even though you are right, nothing will happen because those in charge have either been taken in or intimidated by Greta. It won't be easy to be the first person to stand up to her in your workplace, but once you take the initial steps, you may find that others will follow, albeit perhaps at a distance.

What if your efforts to set limits on your Greta fail or if you are just too intimidated to confront her directly, but you still feel the need to do something concrete to address the problem? To reach that point, one of two things has happened: a major event has led you to conclude that the situation simply cannot continue, or enough small incidents have occurred that you sense a big one is on the way and you need to head it off while you still can.

Before you decide to take action, make sure you can explain to yourself as well as to others what you are concerned about. It need not be a specific action or event—such as, "I'm worried that Greta is stealing from the company." More general concerns, like a lack of teamwork, taking credit for the work of others, lack of civility, and certainly implied or direct threats and general hostility and bullying are all legitimate subjects to be raised. Framing your concerns in the context of the welfare of the organization, rather than "She's picking on me," goes a long way toward capturing the ear of your audience and establishing your reasonableness and credibility.

Next, can you provide evidence to support your concerns? Remember, the almost (or true) psychopath will be glib and charming and have an answer for everything. So unless the person has already lost all credibility, you may find your concerns dismissed out of hand unless you can provide that documentation or at least clear verbal accounts of specific examples. In Greta's case, classmates and co-workers could have kept a running count of her transgressions: snide comments, stolen ideas and boyfriends, excessive charges to the client's account, and mistreatment of colleagues. Any one incident might not be enough to warrant an immediate response, but over time they provide an accurate and disturbing picture of her behavior.

Also consider with whom you are going to raise your concerns. Every organization has policies and procedures for reporting problems with workplace safety, harassment, discrimination, and, increasingly, bullying. Look over your company policies and talk to your human resources rep to learn more, then determine who should hear your complaint. If that person is known to be a close friend of your own Greta, you may need to consider another approach.

Once you have identified whom you will talk to (let's say the HR director), report your concerns to that person and keep track of what you tell him or her and what response you receive. Be aware that confidentiality is unlikely to be an option—assume that Greta will learn who filed the complaint. Keep in mind that there is strength in numbers. If possible, bring a supportive co-worker who shares your views to the meeting, both for verification as well as to keep track of what was said. Don't expect to get more than general support and concern, as opposed to wholesale acceptance of your complaint. Remember, the job of the HR representative is to conduct an objective assessment. If your complaints are about subtle behaviors rather than overt acts of misconduct, frame them in terms of their impact on morale and productivity. Get those concerns on the radar screen of management. Even if the conclusion is that nothing can be done right now, there will be a track record, and eventually it will catch up to the Gretas of the world.

So let's say you have had your meeting with the human resources representative, who listened, nodded at all the appropriate points, encouraged you to share your thoughts and feelings, and promised to look into things. And let's say that after several weeks nothing happens: you get no feedback from HR, and there is no change in Greta's behavior—except maybe you are catching a sarcastic smile or comment more often than before. You are now starting to think that HR and Greta are in cahoots, that she has conned them like everyone else, and that Greta is making plans to make your life miserable. Not so fast. Don't jump to any conclusions. These situations take time, and a good human resources department will be wary of setting itself up for future legal problems, even if the staff have verified your concerns and decided that Greta must go. Yes, it is possible that your paranoia is well-founded, but it is worth checking with HR just to find out where things stand.

If it turns out that your worst suspicions are correct, and if you have the option of leaving, it may be time to buff up your résumé and start the process of moving on to other opportunities. On the other hand, you may learn from HR that things are moving along as quickly as they can, that your patience is appreciated, and that action of some sort is about to be taken.

We like to believe that justice will prevail in these situations, and whether you stay or go, that Greta will get what she deserves—and not what she *thinks* she deserves. However, as we tell our residents, people like Greta are far better at doing what they do than we will ever be in detecting and stopping them. You and your well-being are the top priority. And sometimes that requires that you escape a bad situation and allow others to come to their senses in their own time.

8

Confronting Child Abuse
by Almost Psychopaths

The sexual abuse of children is a horrific and disturbing phenomenon that has occurred throughout history and shows no signs of disappearing in the modern age. At the very least, the perpetrators take advantage of the trusting nature of children (and often their parents), and many times it involves threats of various types or physical violence. Consider the following brief but disturbing examples. They are, unfortunately, true stories; in all of them except the Father John Geoghan story, the names and some details have been changed.

Fred

Becky, a single mother of two, brought her children to the Laundromat. Her hands full with several loads of dirty clothes, not to mention her very bored four- and five-year-old daughters, she appreciated the attention they got from Fred, the friendly man using the washing machines next to her. Like

Becky, Fred was divorced and living alone. He was a bit older and talked about his regret that he and his ex-wife never had children. He mentioned that he loved kids, and it showed as he read to hers, made funny faces, and offered to buy ice cream for everyone. She soon told her family and friends that contrary to her fear that it would never happen, she thought she had met the right guy—someone who was single and liked kids. Over time, the relationship between Becky, her children, and Fred grew stronger.

One day, Fred broke the sad news that he had lost his job and would likely have to move to another state to live with relatives, as he could no longer afford his apartment. Knowing how much she and the girls would miss him, and not wanting to lose this wonderful guy, Becky suggested that he move in with them. Fred agreed "reluctantly" and offered to help take care of the house, mind the children when Becky was at work, and contribute his unemployment check to rent and expenses while he was looking for work. Things went pretty well for about a year, but then Becky noticed a problem—not with Fred, but with her girls. In ways that made Becky stop and take notice, the girls' behavior was changing. They became quieter and withdrawn and a bit oppositional. They were reluctant to be left alone with Fred and seemed angry with her. Not sure what to make of this, and a bit embarrassed that perhaps she was overreacting, Becky mentioned this to the pediatrician during the girls' annual checkup. After a long, private talk with the girls, the pediatrician informed Becky that she, the pediatrician, was obligated to report the family to the Department of Children and Families, a state agency responsible for protecting children from abuse and neglect. The children had revealed that Fred had been climbing into bed with them, peeking at them in the bath, pulling them onto his lap, and had even started touching them in their "private places."

To Becky's horror, she learned that Fred had been telling the girls that his "special attention" was their "secret" and that if they ever told anyone (even each other), people would come and take them away from their family and their mother. During the course of the investigation that immediately followed the pediatrician's report, it became clear that Fred had been grooming the children for sexual abuse since he first met them in the Laundromat. And this wasn't his first time abusing children. He had done the same thing in a prior relationship and had been convicted and served time participating in mandatory therapy. Upon his release, he had moved out of state for a time. When he returned, he registered as a sex offender as required by law. Then he found Becky and her girls.

Dr. Harrison

Dr. Harrison was an esteemed pediatric specialist who received referrals from all of the general pediatricians in town. A clinical faculty member at one of the city's medical schools, he was respected as a teacher and researcher.

Over time, however, troubling rumors began to surface that Dr. Harrison's examinations of his young patients were not quite what they were supposed to be. Operating under the old maxim that "where there's smoke, there's usually fire," a concerned schoolteacher reported the gossip to the state medical board. Once he was officially under investigation, Dr. Harrison gave up his medical license and retired. Several years later, after his premature death, the first of what became a long series of former patients came forth and reported what had happened: for years Dr. Harrison had been conducting unnecessary physical examinations and sexually abusing these children. He did all of this under the guise of a research study, getting consent for multiple examinations of the children. Parents consented because Dr. Harrison claimed to be conducting "research" to try to help other children and their families, and he was meticulously recording data for the "study." The furthest thought from the minds of these parents—or his colleagues—was that this beloved physician, who appeared to be completely devoted to bettering the lives of the young, was actually abusing both children and his position of trust. Dr. Harrison was, in short, brilliant—in a conning and manipulative manner. He deceived the parents, the hospital, and his colleagues, all in order to satisfy his sexual desires.

Father John Geoghan

Although allegations of sexual abuse of children by Catholic priests have become a worldwide scandal, for a time the epicenter of the storm was Boston, Massachusetts. One of the most notorious priests in the Boston scandal was Father John Geoghan. Ordained in 1962, Geoghan eventually admitted to molesting four boys during his assignment to his first parish from 1962 to 1966. The first record of a complaint about Geoghan is from 1968, when a parent complained that he had caught Geoghan molesting his son, but this was far from the last complaint. Salacious allegations followed Geoghan to whichever parish the church assigned him. After the 1968 incident, Church officials forced him to undergo psychiatric treatment at a facility in Baltimore, but Geoghan was soon back at another Massachusetts parish, where one mother alleged he abused all four of her sons. His serial abuse apparently continued throughout the 1970s and 1980s, with Geoghan admitting to some instances of abuse but denying that he had a serious problem. After being ordered to undergo treatment again, this time psychotherapy, Geoghan was soon back at another parish, where a woman complained to Church officials that he had molested her nephew. He apparently continued his pattern unabated, sometimes fondling young boys, one time allegedly raping a fourteen-year-old boy. Geoghan was eventually diagnosed as a pedophile during yet another period of forced treatment in the late 1980s. Church officials finally told him to retire in 1993, and Geoghan became a resident at several retirement homes and treatment centers. His abusive behavior continued, though, and there were multiple additional claims of sexual abuse after 1993.

Some have noted that Geoghan's pattern was to work with boys from poor families, especially those who had experienced recent tragedies and were most in need of "spiritual" support. His abuse of boys in his parishes continued in spite of repeated efforts at both inpatient and outpatient treatment for pedophilia that included psychotherapy as well as psychoanalysis. By 1998, the church had settled fifty sexual abuse cases against Father Geoghan, and eighty-four more were pending. Ultimately, he was the subject of over 130 lawsuits. In 1999, he was indicted in one county in Massachusetts and charged with indecent assault and battery for an incident when he put his hands down the bathing suit of a ten-year-old boy in a swimming pool. He was subsequently indicted in another county on charges of rape and molestation. Geoghan was convicted in 2002 on the molestation charge and received the maximum

sentence while the results of the trial on the rape and molestation charges were still pending. In prison, Geoghan reportedly
denied he had done anything wrong and was considered to
be a problematic inmate. In 2003, he was strangled to death by
another inmate, one who had reportedly been sexually abused
as a child.

Jack

Jack was a high school math teacher and coach of the girls' soc-
cer team. Highly regarded in both capacities, he was a popular
figure about town and seen as a pillar of the community. Even
in this day and age of sordid media accounts of "bad" teachers
who take sexual advantage of their students, parents unques-
tioningly trusted him with their daughters. Married, with a
daughter and two sons, Jack seemed to be the epitome of
a caring teacher who was "all about" the kids.

One spring, a buzz ran through the shocked community.
Shortly after high school commencement, Jack left his wife and
family to live with eighteen-year-old Jennifer, one of his former
players who had just graduated. Other aspects of the scandal
aside, it was highly unlikely that this relationship sprang up
after Jennifer's eighteenth birthday. Both the school and
appropriate social service agencies launched investigations to
determine what had happened and when the relationship had
started. News of the two investigations was of no comfort to
the parents in town. Before the conclusion of either investigation, parents were in an uproar. They no longer wanted Jack
anywhere near their daughters, let alone in the vicinity of the
girls' locker room or supervising them on trips to away games.
Parents besieged school administrators with demands that they

fire Jack, even picketing school committee meetings. Jack also received several anonymous threats over the phone and Internet. Faced with such a passionate response, which he had not foreseen, Jack resigned from both teaching and coaching. In his own mind, though, he couldn't quite understand why everyone was so upset; after all, Jennifer was over eighteen. Eventually it came out that Jack had had his first sexual contact with Jennifer a few months before her sixteenth birthday (the age of consent in their state was sixteen). Jack was subsequently tried and convicted of statutory rape: sexual contact with a person under the age at which the person can give legal consent.

Pedophilia

The term *pedophilia* is well known and in recent years it has been used frequently in the news, usually in connection with horrific stories much like the ones we've presented. Pedophilia is much more common among men, although both case studies and surveys indicate that female pedophiles do exist. In its clinical definition, pedophilia is generally defined as a sexual interest in prepubescent children. One of the sexual and gender identity disorders listed in *DSM–IV–TR*, pedophilia is defined as "recurrent, intense sexually arousing fantasies, sexual urges, or behaviors involving sexual activity with a prepubescent child." The clinical definition is limited to adult and late adolescents, and the sexual urges have been acted on in some way or caused notable distress. (Teens sixteen or older who have relationships with twelve- or thirteen-year-olds are generally not included in the definition.) [74]

Nevertheless, the term is not synonymous with sexual assaults against children. It may seem counterintuitive, but not all pedophiles act on their impulses by attacking children.

In a 2006 survey of men who had committed child pornography offenses—and who are, therefore, considered more likely to be pedophiles—over 50 percent had had no known sexual contact with children.[75] (The survey information was collected from several sources, including criminal records and self-reports.) Not every sexual offense against children will show up in a records check, and it's not difficult to imagine that actual offenders might be reluctant to admit to their conduct. Nevertheless, this survey supports the idea that not everyone who is sexually attracted to children acts on their urges through actual or attempted physical sexual involvement with children.

Conversely, other research suggests that perhaps half of all sexual offenses against children are committed by people who do not fit the diagnostic criteria for pedophilia.[76] Separate studies on the sexual arousal and criminal histories of sex offenders who victimized children showed that approximately 40 to 50 percent of those offenders were *not* pedophiles.[77] There are a variety of reasons why a non-pedophile would commit a criminal offense against a child: lack of sexual opportunities with adults, indiscriminate sexual preferences, and substance abuse resulting in disinhibition, among others.

A Second Look

If, as this research suggests, not all sexual offenses against children are committed by pedophiles, we might want to consider whether other psychological disorders play a role in this criminal behavior. Let's take another look at our examples. All four of the cases we described in this chapter reflect the more common central theme of betrayal of trust, a trait we can also associate with psychopathic behavior, although the cases differ significantly when we examine them more closely.

Fred developed a level of trust with Becky based on what he claimed was his romantic interest, which she reciprocated. Becky's daughters trusted Fred as their new stepfather figure. He duped them all by feigning real affection, part of a deliberate plan to cultivate those relationships for the purpose of grooming the girls to be his next victims. Fred had a criminal history of sexual offending against children and had served time in prison for it. He charmed and manipulated Becky and the girls, as well as Becky's family, to gain complete access to the girls. Given his apparent lack of empathy for the girls and Becky, his repeated criminal behavior, his parasitic lifestyle, and his long-term planning, conning, and manipulation, Fred would receive an elevated score on the PCL–R. It would only require a few more factors, which we would likely find, for us to rate Fred as a full-blown psychopath.

What about Dr. Harrison? From the time of Hippocrates to the modern day, medical professional ethics have required physicians to place the interests and well-being of their patients above all other considerations. In addition, those ethical guidelines have clearly forbidden sexual involvement with patients—not to mention patients who are children. In pursuit of his own desires, Dr. Harrison violated this code of ethics and took advantage of the trust placed in physicians for centuries.

From what we know about Dr. Harrison, he didn't lack empathy—except when it came to his victims. And there was no known evidence of other criminal behavior. He was reportedly regarded as a responsible member of the medical community who served his patients and his community. Unfortunately, he used that position to serve his own psychopathology—his sexual attraction to children, both male and female.

Like Father Geoghan, Dr. Harrison was a pedophile. But did he meet the clinical definition of a psychopath? Perhaps. It is certainly possible that Dr. Harrison went into medicine with the intent of using the profession to gain access to young children. Such long-term scheming would increase the likelihood that he belongs in that category. More likely, though, sometime during his medical career, Dr. Harrison realized that medicine was giving him access to patients who stimulated his sexual desires. It is possible that he knew this was wrong from the beginning, but whether out of fear, embarrassment, or unwillingness to give up the opportunity, he sought no help in setting limits on his own behavior. At some point, however, he was well aware that what he was doing was wrong. Otherwise, why else would he have carried out such an elaborate deception to fulfill his desires? Dr. Harrison's repeated offenses clearly

Can Physicians Be Psychopaths?

We almost instinctively trust anyone who has the ability and who has spent the effort to successfully complete medical school and residency training. Surely, we think, that process must weed out the bad apples. Is it possible, then, that physicians can be psychopaths?

The answer is a definite yes. In fact, a physician was one of Cleckley's original case examples. And physicians can most certainly fall into the almost psychopath range. Both distant and recent history reveal the presence of physicians who were con artists, white-collar criminals committing insurance and disability fraud, serial killers, and sex offenders. Even more common are those physicians who function well in their careers both because and in spite of their psychopathic traits.

mark him as a serial sexual offender, regardless of whether he meets the criteria for true psychopathy. That behavior, the offenses themselves, and his conning and manipulation put him squarely in the almost psychopath category.

Just as we place our faith in our physicians, we trust our religious leaders. Believers and nonbelievers alike tend to venerate these men and women as people who have given up many of the benefits of secular life in order to serve their religion and their congregations. Frequently bright and studious, they are willing to work for far less than they could earn in the secular world, even when they have not taken a vow of poverty.

Geoghan was diagnosed as a pedophile. Based on his history, we have to suspect that his interest in the priesthood was stimulated by the access it would give him to young children. His sexual abuse of children was repetitive, in spite of treatment and the efforts of the church, however weak and ineffective, to curb his behavior. News accounts indicate that in prison Geoghan expressed no remorse and continued to deny that he had done anything wrong. These factors bring his behavior closer to those of a psychopath or almost psychopath.

And what of Jack, the coach who pursued his teenage charge? He certainly violated the community's trust and standards. Where does he fit in this discussion? Whether he is a pedophile will turn on the nature of his attraction to Jennifer. Was he drawn to her because she was a child, or was he attracted to her as a mature, albeit underage, young woman? It is within the realm of possibility that Jack had deep loving feelings for Jennifer that blinded him to the multiple ways in which his involvement with her was unacceptable, both morally and legally. There are certainly questions about the psychological problems that could lead that to happen, but do these actions suggest he is a psychopath? That diagnosis is unlikely, especially if this was the only time he engaged in an inappropriate sexual relationship with a student or other young person. If he and Jennifer go on to have a meaningful relationship, this would further argue against such an assessment. The chances of their having a meaningful relationship, however, are limited, not only by Jack's failure to see what was improper about his behavior, but also by the time he will spend incarcerated for statutory rape.

Violence and sexual abuse can be features of psychopathy. Upon close examination, would we then classify all pedophiles as psychopaths? Unlikely. Again, in placing perpetrators along the almost psychopath continuum, we need to look at the behaviors themselves, the extent to which the perpetrators found their own behavior reprehensible, the level of willingness to get treatment, and the repeated pursuit of the victims. (Of the estimated 50 percent of all sex offenses against children that are not the result of pedophilia, psychopathy is probably a factor; in these cases, the child was likely victimized as a matter of convenience to satisfy the sexual urges of the perpetrator.)

Three of the individuals in our case examples are people who pursued careers that include a commitment to serving others. They were deemed fit to hold the public's trust, often assisting people in their most difficult times. How does someone like that end up committing such acts? It generally starts with a need or desire that the person finds compelling. Their failure to resist that urge may be due to inability or unwillingness, because either they fail to see the need to resist or they just don't want to. And for people holding positions of respect and power, who are given great freedom in their work, the absence of external constraints on their behavior means that there is little to mitigate their lack of self-control.

Most people—even people who do not fall into the range of almost psychopaths—can rationalize their own bad acts. "I'm speeding because I really need to get somewhere fast, and besides I'm a good driver. And the roads are clear." This process of rationalizing can be fueled by what we refer to as *cognitive distortions*—a process by which a person views an event differently from others by virtue of his or her own life experiences, needs, and desires. These cognitive distortions are often self-serving: we tell the story of an event or a thought in a way that makes it acceptable to ourselves and others. In sex offenders, this rationalizing often includes outright denial of the crime, minimization of the harm it has caused, or claims that the victim was a willing participant or actually benefits from the relationship. (One study has indicated that in comparison to nonsexual criminal offenders, rapists separate their own actions from their own professed attitudes. They actually report a higher level of empathy toward women in general and women who have been victims of sexual assault. They just show a deficit in empathy toward their own victims.)[78]

Not all of the men in our examples meet the criteria for psychopathy, but most showed traits that place them somewhere on the spectrum of subclinical psychopathy. The sexual offenses in and of themselves, as reprehensible as they are, do not automatically warrant the title of psychopath for these people, as deeply troubled as they are. However, the repeated pattern of behavior, in known violation of the law and without regard for how it harms the victims, and the use of conning and manipulation, put them well into the almost psychopath category and quite close to full-blown psychopathy. In the case of the Dr. Harrisons of the world, the skill at deceiving whole institutions and communities is as remarkable as it is disturbing.

Is Pedophilia a Mental Disorder?

If pedophilia and the sexual abuse of children don't amount to psychopathy, do they indicate another type of mental illness? There is currently some pressure to include conditions like pedohebephilia (heterosexual attraction of adults to children eleven to fifteen years of age) and ephebophilia (homosexual attraction to children eleven to fifteen years of age) in the *DSM–V.* The seriousness of the problem and society's desire to protect children from being victimized in these ways has also led to the passage of laws that allow for civil commitment of sex offenders to mental hospitals after they have served their criminal sentences. Under these "one day to life" commitments, the "patients" can be released only after they can prove that they are no longer sexually dangerous.

There is some controversy among mental health professionals about this practice, however. Critics maintain that it is unclear whether these people are being confined due to some illness or because they cannot be sentenced to indeterminate prison terms. And as Karen Franklin has pointed out, extensive research has indicated that adult sexual attraction to adolescents is normal.[79] Although pedophilia is listed as a disorder in the *DSM–IV–TR,* the fact that acting out on that attraction is banned by many (but not all) societies makes it a criminal offense, not a mental disorder. Jack, for example, violated the criminal statute that prohibits statutory rape, but one would be hard-pressed to describe him as mentally ill and a candidate for civil, as opposed to criminal, commitment in a mental health facility.

What to Do?

How is it that people are able to abuse children repeatedly, often over years or decades? Various explanations have been offered, including ignorance of how much harm it causes, shame or embarrassment in addressing the abuse, and refusal to believe that a person we know or who has respected status in society could commit such an act. The failure of individuals in positions of authority to intervene when reports of sexual abuse are raised is shameful, and many institutions have paid a severe price—although the price paid by the child victims is far higher.

The most important step toward ending this abuse is what we call *primary prevention:* making sure the injury never occurs. First and foremost, if you or anyone you know is feeling sexual urges toward children, know that there is help. While the effectiveness of various approaches is somewhat controversial, there is evidence that treatment can be effective in motivated individuals, and even if the urge has been acted upon, it can reduce the chance of a repeat offense.[80]

Treatment, however, is not always effective. Perpetrators are not always willing to seek help, and there are psychopaths and almost psychopaths who prey on children. How do we protect our children? And how do we do so without becoming mistrusting of every individual and person in their lives?

To start with, it is important to combine our inherently trusting natures with a bit of suspicion regarding those who care for and interact with our children. If you are in the position of Becky—lonely, wanting a partner to help raise your children and be in your life—it is important to be aware that while Prince (or Princess) Charming can indeed come along, sometimes things are too good to be true. Before getting into a relationship that may put your child at risk, check out the details about this person's life. (Is this romantic? Of course not, but the safety of your children may be at stake.) Find out if your state, city, or town has a registry of sex offenders, and if there is one, check it. Depending on where you live, locating this registry might be as simple as accessing a website or calling the local police station. (One national resource is the Dru Sjodin National Sex Offender Public Website at www.nsopw.gov.) Even if the process is more complicated, the effort may well be worth it. Had Becky done that, an enormous amount of heartache would have been avoided.

When it comes to teachers, coaches, health care workers, and others with access to children, communities have become much more diligent about background checks, including review of sex offender registries, before allowing unsupervised contact with children. That's a good start, but our caution shouldn't stop there. Get to know the people who are going to work with your child and ask about their backgrounds and their life histories—it will help you connect with them and also let you look for inconsistencies or problems. Talk to your children about their interactions with their coach or teacher, and compare notes with other parents and share your impressions and what you have learned.

And most important, educate your children that their bodies belong to them, that parts of their body are private, that no one has a right to touch them in a way that makes them uncomfortable, and that they can say no if anyone—an adult or another child—touches them in a way they don't like. Make sure they know that it is okay to come to you when they feel uncomfortable in any way. The psychopaths and almost psychopaths of the world are a minority of our population, but the risk remains high and the importance of preventing further victimization demands that we do everything we can to protect our children.

9

Adults as Victims
Confronting Almost Psychopaths
in the Helping Professions

As we saw in the previous chapter, sometimes those whom we trust can break that trust in one of the most horrible ways possible: abusing children. However, it's not just children who can be taken advantage of. Adults can also become the victims of the unscrupulous and psychopathic behavior of the very people whom they believed could and would help them. Trust is the foundation of professional relationships. It can also be the gateway for almost psychopaths to enter our lives and create painful chaos.

George

After George and his wife went through a difficult period in their marriage, George decided to enter psychotherapy. After only a few meetings, the therapist suggested that George's wife, Ann, come in for a few sessions, and she agreed. After two sessions, the therapist began seeing them as a couple. Initially, there seemed to be some progress; Ann seemed happier at home and she was invested in the therapy. Which made it all the more shocking when one day Ann announced that the marriage was over and she wanted her husband out of the house. Devastated, George called his therapist in a panic, and the therapist agreed to see him that day. The therapist was supportive but told George that "sometimes things turn out this way, and it's probably best for you to move on with your life." In short order, the couple divorced. Some months later, George learned that Ann and his therapist (who was still treating George!) were living together.

Amanda

Amanda was a bright fourteen-year-old from a small-town family that could best be described as high pressure. Following in the footsteps of her older siblings, Amanda was a high achiever, but her energy was fueled by low self-esteem and her fear of not living up to what her brother and sister had accomplished. In high school, she joined the cross country and track teams, running endless miles and losing weight, trying to minimize her body fat. Eventually, her parents noted that she was losing more and more weight. When they commented on it, she protested that she was "too fat" and needed to lose more.

Diagnosed with an eating disorder, Amanda got into treatment, did well in high school, and headed off to college. Away from home, though, she had difficulty adjusting, her eating disorder returned, and she had to drop out of school. Rather than go back home, she took a job in the city where her college was located, in order to be close to the therapist she had been seeing. Over the course of the next year, Amanda began to experience a variety of medical problems related to her eating disorder. Her therapist referred her to Dr. Smith, a primary care physician who had worked with the therapist's patients with eating disorder in the past.

Amanda became very attached to Dr. Smith, telling him that he was the only doctor who had ever understood her and asking to see him more frequently (which was justified by her worsening medical problems) and for longer visits. When her therapist retired, Amanda asked Dr. Smith if she could see him for counseling as well as her medical issues. He agreed; he was proud to be able to help such a troubled young patient and to be the "only one" who could connect with her. Besides, he had taken a psychiatry rotation in medical school and had briefly considered going into that specialty.

Over time, Amanda's appointments with Dr. Smith became more frequent and longer. Rather than the usual fifteen- to twenty-minute primary care visits, he saw her for a combined medical checkup and "counseling" session that lasted fifty to sixty minutes—a standard psychotherapy visit. Playing the role of therapist, Dr. Smith did what he had been taught psychiatrists do—talk to patients about their childhood and their relationships. Through a combination of his mistaken notions of therapy and Amanda's desire to please him, their work began to include discussion of childhood trauma, fueled in part by something he read about "regression therapy"—a dubious treatment in which patients are encouraged to reexperience their childhood in order to address their issues from that time. During these sessions, Amanda ended up sitting on Dr. Smith's lap as he read her children's books. In spite of the supposed therapeutic nature of the encounters, they quickly became sexualized, and Amanda began getting worse instead of better —reacting with severe depression when Dr. Smith said he could not see her or he cut short their appointments. When Dr. Smith came to his senses and broke off the relationship, Amanda attempted suicide. The nature of her relationship with Dr. Smith was revealed during her subsequent inpatient treatment, and his behavior was reported to the Board of Medicine, which started an investigation. Amanda eventually sued Dr. Smith for malpractice.

Eva

After being badly injured in a car accident, Eva did what lots of people do—she hired a lawyer and sued the driver of the other car. She won, and the jury awarded her a substantial judgment with the payments going initially into a trust account that the lawyer maintained and then to her.

At first, the system went like clockwork; on the first of every month, Eva received her check. But suddenly the payments stopped. Eva repeatedly called her lawyer, Janice, to ask what was going on. Janice explained that there was a paperwork snafu, but she could pay a partial amount. From then on, the payments to Eva came only sporadically, and Eva continued to besiege Janice with calls. Eventually, Janice stopped answering. Eva filed a complaint with the state bar association and learned that Janice had used her money, and the money of other clients, to cover some bad investments she had made. The sad truth was that Janice was broke. Fortunately, the state bar association maintained an account for just this sort of situation (this was not the first time an attorney had done something like this), and Eva received a small portion of her money.

Margaret

At age eighty-two, Margaret finally acknowledged that she could no longer take care of herself without help. Unwilling to go into a nursing home, she decided to use her substantial financial assets to arrange for round-the-clock care in her own home. Although she suffered from arthritis, a weakening heart, and the early stages of dementia, she still enjoyed her garden and her own rooms. Her accountant assured her that she had plenty of money to pay for the live-in assistance and still have funds to leave to her beloved nephews and her favorite charity.

Through her church, Margaret found Lina, a registered nurse who ran a home care service. Lina agreed to have people on her staff assist Margaret. This worked well for a while, but as Margaret's dementia got worse, Lina offered to move in with Margaret full time and become her personal caretaker, with additional staff coming in only occasionally. Margaret had grown quite fond of Lina, who had also earned the trust of Margaret's nephews, Dave and Greg. The nephews, both in their mid-sixties with health problems of their own, lived out of town but took turns visiting Margaret monthly.

After Lina moved in, things changed. She took very good care of Margaret, but when Dave and Greg called, Lina told them that Margaret couldn't come to the phone because she was sleeping or not feeling well. When they came to see Margaret, Lina hovered nearby and kept the visits short, saying it was just "doctor's orders." At the same time, she was cutting off Greg's and Dave's access to their aunt, Lina was telling

Margaret, whose memory was failing steadily, that Dave and Greg were so busy with other "more important" things that they had to keep their visits short. She also lied and told Margaret that no one from her favorite charity had called or written. Finally, Lina asked Margaret to hire Lina's daughter, Agnes, to provide some of the care. She explained that Agnes was a single mother of two children who had been abandoned by her husband. Margaret agreed. After all, Agnes was so sweet, and it was such a sad story. And besides, Lina pointed out, Agnes was so caring, not like those nephews of hers or the people from the charity who seemed to be forgetting about Margaret.

Before long, when Margaret was totally dependent on Lina and Agnes, Lina suggested to Margaret that she might want to change her will to help those who were most devoted to her. Lina brought in another relative of hers who was an attorney. He drafted a new will for Margaret that left a tiny percentage of the estate to Dave and Greg, cut out the charity entirely, and left the rest to Lina and Agnes.

The Importance of Boundaries

Before we turn to examining each of these cases in more detail, let's consider what they have in common. All of them reflect breaches of professional ethics. But, perhaps more fundamentally, they all involve violations and abuse of the trust that people need to have in the professionals who serve them. As discussed in the previous chapter, trust makes it possible for us to send our children to school, to be examined by health care professionals, and to be under the tutelage of coaches. And once that trust regarding the proper care of our children is established, it can be exploited by the unscrupulous. The same is true when it comes to relationships between professionals and their adult patients and clients.

An essential part of developing and maintaining that trust is the establishment and preservation of appropriate *boundaries* in the patient/client-practitioner relationship. What defines appropriate boundaries in these relationships depends to a degree upon the ethical standards set by each profession, the nature of the activity, and the context in which the relationship occurs. A physician's examination of a patient's body, especially breasts and genitals, necessarily involves physical contact that in other contexts would be considered sexual. But the setting or context—the bright lights of an examination room and not the subdued lighting of a bedroom—and the manner of touch— purposeful and direct rather than caressing—make it clear that this is about medical care, not lust or romance. Yet the difference between clinical and sexual touch can easily be misperceived unless meticulous boundaries are maintained.

Similarly, in the discussion of intimate personal matters that occurs during psychotherapy, patients often develop strong feelings of attachment and affection for the therapist. Those feelings, along with any others that the patient has for the therapist (favorable or unfavorable), are referred to as *transference*, as they reflect the transfer of feelings that the patient has had for other people in his or her life to the therapist. Therapists also have emotional reactions to their patients, referred to as *countertransference*, which likewise reflects the therapist's own life experiences and interactions with others.

Most people think the concepts of transference and counter-transference only apply to mental health professionals, but these phenomena take place all the time and in every relationship, including those featured in our case examples. These interactions are more highly charged, however, and have greater implications in professional interactions where physical and emotional intimacy may be interpreted as romantic attraction, rather than as a by-product of the professional relationship.

The professional is responsible for recognizing and managing the transference and countertransference in the professional relationship. When the therapist/physician fails to do that, both the professional and the patient may start to believe that what they are feeling is "true love," which, like other intoxicants, can lead to disinhibition and impaired judgment. And that, in turn, can lead to boundary crossings (relatively minor breaches) and full-blown violations of appropriate professional boundaries.

While we tend to focus on maintaining appropriate physical and emotional boundaries, others are also essential to creating and maintaining healthy relationships between professionals and their clients or patients. These include using the patients' information only for their benefit, rather than that of the professionals. Receiving gifts from clients is another potential boundary issue. Is there an absolute prohibition? No, but as the size of the gift or the degree of the patient's impairment increases, the ethical challenges surrounding gift giving and receiving grow.

Professionals and those they serve need to be aware of both crossings and violations of appropriate professional boundaries. As noted above, crossings are relatively mild transgressions that can and should be addressed. Depending on the setting and context, these can include instances where the professional shares too much personal information about his or her own life problems with a patient so that they end up talking more about the professional's difficulties than the patient's. Boundary violations are those over-the-top events in which appropriate boundaries are clearly transgressed at great potential harm to the client or patient. Our examples all concern major boundary violations, from sexual contact with a patient and with a patient's spouse, to "borrowing" the patient's funds from the trust account, to manipulating the patient's affections in order to have her alter her estate plan.

Violating Boundaries

The case of George and his therapist and that of Amanda and Dr. Smith represent two different examples of the same problem: sexual misconduct by a treating clinician. In the first case, not only did the therapist betray George by having an affair with his wife; he also accepted Ann as a patient in couples' treatment and then had a sexual relationship with her. The ethical standards concerning therapist-client relationships vary across the major professional organizations. The American Psychiatric Association says that it's unethical for a psychiatrist to *ever* have sexual involvement with a patient or *former* patient: the basic idea is "once a patient, always a patient." On the other hand, the American Psychological Association holds that a psychologist can have a sexual relationship with a former patient as long as it starts no sooner than two years after termination of the treatment relationship. In George's case, however, it doesn't matter which standard we look to. The therapist clearly violated both standards.

The situation with Amanda and Dr. Smith is an example of

a slightly different boundary violation. While some clinicians who engage in boundary violations are sexual predators, the majority of sexual misconduct cases involve middle-age or older male professionals with stagnated marriages and/or careers or who have had other losses and who find themselves treating a patient they find attractive and who reveres them and listens to what they have to say. This engenders very positive feelings for the clinician, and those emotions feel like love. (While the majority of these cases involve a male clinician and a female patient, we also see cases involving every other gender combination of clinician and patient). From the information available, it appears Dr. Smith's case may be like these instances of clinician sexual misconduct.

What about Amanda's behavior? She's an adult after all. Shouldn't she be at least partly responsible for enticing Dr. Smith into that relationship? No. It is always the responsibility of the clinician to maintain appropriate boundaries, no matter what the patient says or does. In psychotherapy (and remember, Dr. Smith was offering his services as a psychotherapist), any sexual involvement with a patient is both a breach of ethics and a violation of the standard of care. It is a basis for losing the license to practice medicine and other clinical professions in all states, and in over twenty states it is a criminal offense for physicians of all types—not only psychiatrists or psychotherapists.

Was Dr. Smith an almost psychopath? Barring any evidence that he has regularly behaved this way or exhibits other behaviors and characteristics on the psychopathy checklists, the answer would be no, at least based on the information we have. He certainly breached professional standards and caused Amanda substantial harm. But he did so as a result of his lack

ADULTS AS VICTIMS ❖

of expertise and because he managed a difficult patient very poorly and did not recognize the feelings in their relationship for what they were. That makes him a legitimate candidate for a malpractice suit and loss of his license to practice, but not necessarily for almost psychopath status.

Can we say that George's therapist was an almost (or full-blown) psychopath? Not with the information we have. As with our earlier examples, we would have to know a bit more about the therapist and his prior behavior.

Further complicating matters, the professional standards around therapist conduct have evolved relatively recently. Until the 1980s, some members of the mental health professions saw sexual involvement with their patients as one of the benefits of their work. In fact, some even argued that because of their superior knowledge and understanding, they had the ability to use this sexual involvement therapeutically to help the patient. Some of these people were true predators, but the majority actually believed this argument or otherwise rationalized their behavior. Compiling a list of candidates for almost (or true) psychopath status, we would have to include those therapists who engaged in this behavior and then denied the allegations, saying the patient had an "erotic transference" or was psychotic. More commonly, therapists like the one in George's case fall into the category inhabited by Dr. Smith, people whose behavior may be unethical, even technically criminal in some states, but represents psychological problems other than psychopathy.

Our lawyer, Janice, committed one of the most serious, and most common, breaches of attorney professional responsibility: comingling of assets. In fact, the problem is so common that states establish funds to compensate victims of unscrupulous attorneys. How does someone who works so hard to pass the bar examination and is sworn in as an attorney come to decide it is okay to use her client's money to pay her own bills? Well, remember what we said about rationalization: even normal people can rationalize their moral gaps, their actions that arise because of their moral blind spots or superego lacunae. The more frequent this ethical violation and the greater the amounts of money involved, the more likely the attorney qualifies as an almost psychopath. In the cases that we are familiar with, factors such as substance abuse, bipolar disorder, or depression have played a significant role in the attorney's impaired judgment.

While there are attorneys who view the client's trust account as their personal piggy bank (and these are the attorneys who qualify as almost psychopaths), they represent the minority in such cases. More commonly, when money has been misappropriated by a legal adviser, the attorney has had some significant life stresses—personal, financial, or both—and feels the need for more cash or the lawyer's judgment has been impaired by substance abuse or illness. He or she rationalizes that the money will be returned shortly—"It is only a short-term loan" or "Taking it is not like 'stealing' because the money is just sitting there and once it's paid back, no one will ever know it went missing." But then something happens, and the money can't be paid back, which perhaps leads to "borrowing" from another client's account. This pattern continues on an increasingly slippery slope, until one or more clients realize what has been happening, resulting not only in the client's loss but almost certain devastation of a legal career and possible incarceration.

But how should we understand Lina and Margaret's story? Cases like these come to our attention in two ways. In some, concerned family members become suspicious of the newcomer's influence and ask for an assessment of the situation, including an evaluation of the patient's capacity to make important decisions. In others, the issue does not arise until after the patient dies and the will is read. Those who expected to inherit find themselves left out in favor of strangers. The will

Who's Really What?

There is another level of deception that almost psychopaths may stoop to in the professional arena: they may not even *be* the professionals they claim to be. Almost psychopaths are often accomplished liars whose boldness, in some ways, gives them the credibility to pull off their deceit. Some may simply falsify their education and make up degrees. The Internet makes it easier than ever for them to actually purchase authentic-looking credentials from *degree mills* that confer diplomas with little or no work. Ironically, the explosion of online education from reputable colleges and universities is giving cover to those who are looking to buy an edge in a competitive job market, as well as those who are bent on conning their way into a life they haven't earned and don't deserve.

The consequences can be devastating. In 1999, Marion Kolitwenzew took her diabetic daughter to a specialist, who advised that she take her daughter off insulin. In part because of the impressive-looking degrees in the specialist's office, Kolitwenzew followed the advice. Her eight-year-old daughter died as a result. The "specialist's" degrees were from a degree mill, and he was eventually convicted of manslaughter. If he was an almost psychopath, he likely didn't even feel guilty about the incalculable damage he had caused.

is then challenged on two possible grounds: lack of testamentary capacity (the person didn't really understand the purpose of the document he or she signed, the extent of the estate, or who normally would have inherited from him or her) or undue influence (the person made changes to the will that he or she wouldn't have made without pressure from someone who stands to benefit from the changes). In this case, Lina acted in a predatory manner—realizing that she could take advantage of Margaret's trust and debilitated state and use them to her and her daughter's financial advantage, without regard to the impact on Margaret, her nephews, and the beneficiaries of the charity that would have inherited a portion of the estate. The manipulative touch that most impressed us in the real-world case of Lina was her bringing in a relative as the attorney and another who would benefit from Lina's influence over Margaret and her incapacity. Is Lina, then, an almost psychopath? Yes (unless further investigation shows that she meets the full criteria for psychopathy).

How to Protect Yourself

How might you protect yourself from predatory therapists or physicians? If you are George, you can file a complaint with the state agency that licenses your therapist and seek justice in the legal system. By making this effort, you may be saving another person from having the same experience you had. That therapist—if his misconduct with clients is part of a pattern—may well be a psychopath, or at the very least an almost psychopath, and he or she will almost certainly reoffend, given the opportunity.

If you are a patient of a therapist like Dr. Smith, please keep the following in mind. The feelings you have for your clinician may well feel like "true love." Setting aside the complex question of what true love is, consider that those feelings are likely the product of transference. Those feelings are normal, and talking about them with your therapist can lead to significant progress in treatment. Tell your therapist about them. A competent therapist will respond supportively, assuring you that this is normal and encouraging you to talk about it more. But if the clinician talks about sharing those feelings of attraction and indicates an interest in pursuing them both emotionally and physically, beware. This could be an intentional manipulation of you and your clinical needs by a predator who is an almost psychopath. In this case, leave the treatment, seek help elsewhere, and consider filing a complaint with the appropriate licensing authority.

If you have concerns about what is going on in your therapy, consider contacting TELL, the Therapy Exploitation Link Line, at www.therapyabuse.org. TELL responders, all of whom have suffered abuse by therapists, can help you think through what is happening and take appropriate action.

More likely, the clinician's response is not intentional manipulation but represents the negligent handling of your treatment by someone who is struggling with his or her own psychological problems. If there are mutual feelings or if the relationship has become physical, insist that you and the therapist each consult with respected members of the clinical community about what to do with the treatment. Almost always, it will be best to end the treatment immediately and find another clinician, although some cases are more complicated and require a more gradual termination, with supervision of that process.

In the case of physicians or therapists like Dr. Smith, they also should be reported to the appropriate licensing board, and a malpractice suit may be appropriate. The decision to do either of those things is often difficult, however, especially when the patient has developed a strong emotional attachment to the clinician. In Dr. Smith's case, there is a fair chance that the behavior was the product of psychological problems that can be addressed, so long as the clinician acknowledges that the behavior is inappropriate and wants to get help.

If you are a clinician and find yourself developing strong feelings of love or lust for your patient, are considering entering into a business relationship with a patient, or are facing any

The "Clinicide" Phenomenon

Every breach of trust by a doctor should be taken seriously, and a pattern could very well be an indication that the doctor is an almost psychopath. Even so, some ethical violations by doctors are more dangerous than others. Consider the relatively unexplored phenomenon of clinicide, defined as the unnatural death of patients who are receiving treatment from a particular doctor. While controversial and considered unethical in most places, assisted suicide or euthanasia of a terminally ill and suffering patient generally do not necessarily indicate that the doctor is an almost or a true psychopath. On the other hand, some clinicidal doctors seem to have extreme narcissistic personalities—the full-blown "God complex"—that leads them to believe that they have the right to decide whether someone lives or dies.[81] Doubtless, some of these doctors also have psychopathic traits that allow them to ignore the needs of the patient and the emotional toll on the patient's family and friends.

one of the numerous potential boundary-crossing/violation scenarios, stop! This is the sort of situation that cries out for the motto popularized by our colleague Dr. Thomas Gutheil: Never worry alone. The more you keep your concerns or actions to yourself and maintain that secret, the harder it will be to address the question later. The fact that you have initial qualms is a good sign that your ethical and moral instincts are correct, and now is the time to act on that. Doing so will save you, your patient, and your loved ones a great deal of heartache and perhaps save your career.

. . .

Now, how can you protect yourself against professionals who abuse your trust and misappropriate money? What can you do about lawyers like Janice? The best thing in this case is prevention. A good first step anytime you are considering retaining an attorney, even for what might seem like a relatively straightforward problem, is to do a little research. Check with the local and state bar associations to see if there have been any complaints again your potential lawyer. Then move on to the next step: ask the hard questions. Even if you are familiar with your potential attorney, or the person is recommended by a friend or family member, ask how your funds will be handled and ask for regular accountings. If you discover a problem, insist that it be corrected immediately and give serious thought to reporting the incident to the bar in your state. This may not be the first such complaint against your attorney.

People who are elderly and disabled, like Margaret, are particularly attractive targets for the almost psychopaths and true psychopaths of the world. These individuals are often lonely and frightened by their advancing age and illness, and their emotions are easily manipulated by people who know how to feign concern and caring, and how to insinuate themselves into the lives of people like Margaret.

Margaret and others in her position, however, are entitled to change their minds about their estate plans and to whom they want to leave their money. They have a right to reward those who devote time to them in their waning years. In fact, the standard for testamentary capacity is fairly low, in part because society believes that people should have a right to determine how their property will be distributed upon their death. But just because they have the right to change their minds doesn't mean that they weren't duped by an almost psychopath taking advantage of their declining mental faculties and desire for companionship in their remaining years.

Family members or others who care for an individual and are in a position to do so should assist their own "Margaret" in the hiring of a caregiver. This includes asking for and following up on references, interviewing applicants, and checking with state agencies for appropriate licenses and any history of complaints. Health care proxies and durable powers of attorney are useful in making sure that a responsible and reliable person will be making decisions on behalf of the person when he or she becomes sufficiently incapacitated. Obviously, these should be in place before the disability progresses so far that the person is no longer capable of making rational decisions.

Once a caregiver is in place, family members and friends should take note if access to their loved one is being restricted. If the caregiver tells you that "the doctor" said no visitors, call the doctor and ask if this is true. If you have been designated as the agent under the health care proxy, or the patient has otherwise designated you as one with whom information can be shared, the doctor will talk to you. Regardless, the rules of confidentiality do not prevent the physician from *receiving* information, just from releasing it without authorization. Even if you are not legally authorized to receive information, you can still pass along your concerns that the patient is being confined and isolated. In addition, you can consider reporting your concerns to state social service agencies that are responsible for investigating cases of elder abuse.

We'll close this chapter as we started, emphasizing the importance of trust in professional relationships but noting that trust is a double-edged sword. The same things that make trust possible, and essential, provide an opportunity for almost psychopaths to take advantage of what should be honorable, caring, and rewarding relationships.

| 10 |

Sick or Slick?
Malingering and Manipulation of Illness

All of us get sick at some point. If we are lucky, the illness is
minor. But, of course, sometimes it's serious, leading to disability, lost income, and enormous medical bills. Workers' compensation, disability, and health insurance were developed to
help people get through these difficult times. If those systems
fail, communities often step up to help out their friends and
neighbors. But when there are benefits to be had and helping
hands to be offered, often there will be almost psychopaths
and true psychopaths to take advantage. Consider our next case
examples (but beware: the third case is not for the squeamish).

Bob
Bob started out as a paperboy when he was in elementary
school and continued working various jobs before starting at a
local manufacturing plant right after graduation from high
school. The work was hard—lots of employees didn't last six

months—but Bob kept at it and eventually secured a salaried middle management position with a full slate of benefits, including excellent long-term disability coverage.

One Saturday, Bob took his car to a service center to have the tires rotated. On his way home, one of the wheels came flying off, sending the car into a ditch where it came to a screeching halt in a grove of small trees. A passing driver called in the accident. When the emergency medical technicians (EMTs) arrived, they found Bob still in the driver's seat of the damaged car. Bob was staring straight ahead with now-deflated airbags resting on his lap, and he wasn't able to move his arms or legs. Obviously concerned, the EMTs worked deliberately and carefully as they maneuvered him onto a backboard and into the ambulance.

At the hospital, Bob gradually began to move his arms and legs but spoke only in grunts and groans, pointing to things he wanted. The doctors ordered a head computerized tomography (CT) scan and other radiologic studies but found nothing that could explain his apparent cognitive difficulties. Eventually, Bob was sent home with plans for outpatient physical and cognitive rehabilitation.

Bob was diligent in following the treatment plans but showed only gradual improvement in his puzzling cognitive impairment. He was in no condition to return, even part time, to work. His clinicians disagreed about whether this was the result of a traumatic brain injury or was some sort of psychological problem, so they decided to watch and see how he did as he continued with treatment. In his rehabilitation efforts, Bob showed a strange pattern of difficulties, with poor motor coordination and slurred speech. At times he seemed to have memory problems, although puzzled staff members noted that he was the only one on the unit who could use the remote control on the new TV. And no one could quite figure out why he had lost control of his bladder function and was periodically incontinent. While the pattern of his impairments was strange, his doctors ultimately were convinced that Bob was impaired and signed off on the disability forms to his work and the long-term disability insurance company. He would now receive 65 percent of his full salary, tax free, plus all of his benefits.

But this wasn't the only disability payment that Bob was receiving. He had bought two private disability policies, small enough that when he purchased them no red flags had been raised. And Bob certainly didn't tell his employer or their disability insurer. In fact, no one but Bob knew about the additional policies, until a routine visit to Bob's home by a disability company case manager raised some questions.

The home was neat and clean when Bob's wife welcomed the case manager and brought him to the living room. Soon Bob came down the stairs, lurching along and almost, but not quite, falling. He greeted the case manager with his usual grunting sounds and then collapsed—carefully—into a chair. Bob made a big show of lifting his leg and putting it on the coffee table, displaying the urine collection bag that was attached to his leg. The bag was brand new and contained no urine—nor did it ever collect any over the case manager's two-hour visit. The case manager thought that was odd, knowing that if it were actually connected, it should have collected something in that time.

Because of this and a "gut feel," the case manager suggested that Bob's case get a closer look. The first step was to bring in an outside medical consultant to review Bob's record, which raised more concerns about Bob's inconsistent physical and cognitive problems. The consultant suggested that Bob be admitted to an inpatient rehabilitation unit where he could be observed constantly and undergo a complete, extended assessment. As the consultant had expected, the constant observation, as well as careful assessment, revealed that Bob was feigning his symptoms. The staff noted that Bob's physical impairments seemed to disappear when he thought he wasn't being observed, and his neuropsychological testing revealed obvious inconsistencies, with Bob failing the simple tests and acing the harder ones.

Based on the findings from the inpatient stay, the insurance company notified Bob that it was suspending disability payments to him while it reviewed his case. Bob and his wife retained an attorney, who promptly brought a claim against the insurer. As part of its investigation, the insurer set up video surveillance of Bob. While this tactic may sound over the top and unnecessarily invasive, it is a common practice among disability insurers who are very keen on weeding out false claims. What did this surveillance reveal? Bob—supposedly physically and cognitively impaired, incontinent, and unable to care for himself—was filmed lifting his four-year-old grandson into a van, getting into the driver's seat, and taking the boy apple picking. Confronted with this evidence, Bob withdrew his case against the insurer and declared bankruptcy in an effort to avoid having to return the money he had already been paid.

Connie

Connie volunteered at the local hospital and served as a crossing guard at the neighborhood elementary school. With no children of her own, she was very fond of the kids she saw every day, always greeting them and their parents with a smile and wave. It was with great sadness that word spread through the community that Connie had cancer.

Lymphoma, people said. Or leukemia. One of those—it didn't really matter. The important thing was that this sweet person, who was so kind to the children, was sick. So sick, in fact, that she couldn't be treated at the local hospital but instead had to travel by plane to an academic medical center where she could see a cancer specialist for experimental treatments. People became used to Connie and her husband being out of town for a week or two at a time. When she was in town, people saw her with her head wrapped in a scarf or wearing a hat—to cover up her hair loss from chemo, they thought. Other than her apparent hair loss, Connie looked pretty good. She would come back from many of her trips looking, well, tan. A side effect of the chemo, she told people when they commented. In these casual conversations, Connie also let it be known that she and her husband were running out of money. The experimental treatment wasn't covered by their health insurance, and they were paying out of pocket. Add to that the cost of the plane tickets, hotels, meals, her husband's lost income . . . . Well, she was going to have to stop treatment and let the cards fall where they may. As soon as word got around, people in Connie's town stepped right up. There was no way they were going to let her down when she was in such great need. Within weeks, major fund-raising efforts were under way to support Connie. There were bake sales, silent auctions, charity basketball games—you name it. The community turned out and donated both time and money. Over the course of several months, the community raised nearly $25,000, giving all of it to Connie and her husband. Soon Connie seemed to improve a bit, even putting on some weight and sporting a more consistently even tan when she returned from her time away for "chemo."

As her condition seemed to improve, or at least grow no worse, a number of Connie-skeptics popped up. People began to ask questions about her treatment and that tan. There was a growing sense that something was up, but what? To most, Connie was her old sweet self and what a fighter! But others started to openly ask, how could she look so good while still supposedly being so sick?

The mystery was solved when a family who lived on Connie's street returned from Disney World with their children and reported that they had seen Connie (and her husband) there— and Connie, with plenty of hair, was working on her tan at the pool. Connie, who was supposed to be at chemo, didn't have cancer. She wasn't sick at all. While they were still in Florida, Connie and her husband learned that they were in trouble— angry e-mails and texts flooded their accounts. The next time they came home, it was to stand trial for fraud and theft.

Sally

Sally was a "frequent flyer" at the emergency room for a wide variety of symptoms. She presented with multiple, diffuse aches and pains, but not much else—lots of subjective complaints but no objective findings. She was regarded as a "crock," a patient who presents with made-up or exaggerated complaints, and the residents in the emergency room quickly tired of her. Occasionally, a less experienced resident would decide that Sally had some exotic illness. (In evaluating her odd symptoms they were ignoring the diagnostic advice we mentioned earlier: they heard hoofbeats and were thinking of zebras, rather than horses.) But once results from the tests and sometimes invasive procedures came back, these residents lost interest as well. Sally seemed to be aware that inexperience was her ally; her visits to the emergency room ran in spurts—a big surge in July when the new medical residents started and then smaller jumps when their rotations changed.

One July, Sally arrived in the ER complaining of pain in her abdomen. The triage nurse, who knew Sally well, rolled her eyes but took her vital signs. This time, Sally's temperature was 101 degrees and her pulse rate was higher than usual. The first-year resident assigned to Sally took a careful history and then began the examination. She noticed immediately that Sally had several large, inflamed bumps on her abdomen—abscesses. Blood tests revealed that Sally had all the signs of infection, and the infection had spread to her bloodstream, referred to as *sepsis*. The blood and skin cultures revealed that a type of bacteria normally found in the gastrointestinal tract was causing these abscesses. Strange, but not unheard of. Although skin abscesses are normally treated on an outpatient basis, Sally was admitted to the hospital because of the sepsis and the possibility that something else was going on that was suppressing her immune system. A workup for immune deficiency problems, which could have explained the abscesses and sepsis, was negative.

Sally responded well to intravenous antibiotics and surgical treatment of the abscesses, which proved to be quite deep.

Shortly before she was to be discharged, Sally spiked a temperature. Examination indicated that the original abscesses had largely healed, but now they had appeared on her left thigh. Puzzled, Sally's doctors reevaluated her for immune deficiency and again found nothing. They requested her permission to get her medical records from other hospitals, but Sally claimed she had never been treated anywhere else. Review of her outpatient records showed a large number of complaints and higher-than-normal demand for attention, but nothing like this.

The treatment team became suspicious that perhaps Sally was causing these infections herself. How else were bacteria from the gastrointestinal tract getting into the skin of her abdomen—all on the left side of her body—without an anatomical problem that would allow the bacteria to escape from her gastrointestinal tract? One day, while Sally was off the unit for some tests, her treatment team searched her room and found syringes and needles that Sally had been using to inject feces into her skin to cause the abscesses. When her doctors showed Sally what they had found, she insisted on signing out against medical advice, refusing the offer of psychological help.

Faking It: Feigning Illness

As we have noted, at one time or another, most of us have exaggerated a minor illness in order to get sympathy from a loved one, such as a spouse or parent, or even to avoid some responsibility. Even if we were kids the last time we did it, it's not uncommon for people to play up an illness to get a break on an exam or to get a day off from work to attend an afternoon baseball game. Are all the people who played hooky in this way almost psychopaths? Of course not. But some are.

Faking an illness for personal gain is called *malingering*, and it has been part of cultures around the world throughout history. Malingering is not considered a mental disorder, although it is listed in the *DSM–IV–TR* as one of the "V" codes: "other conditions that may be the focus of clinical attention." Some people malinger in order to avoid obligations such as military service or work. And when compensation is available for an injury—as in a personal injury lawsuit, disability

What Is Malingering?

The *DSM–IV–TR* describes malingering as follows:

The essential feature of Malingering is the intentional production of false or grossly exaggerated physical or psychological symptoms, motivated by external incentives such as avoiding military duty, avoiding work, obtaining financial compensation, evading criminal prosecution, or obtaining drugs. Under some circumstances, Malingering may represent adaptive behavior—for example, feigning illness while a captive of the enemy during wartime.

Malingering should be strongly suspected if any combination of the following is noted:

1. Medicolegal context of presentation (e.g., the person is referred by an attorney to the clinician for examination)
2. Marked discrepancy between the person's claimed stress or disability and the objective findings
3. Lack of cooperation during the diagnostic evaluation and in complying with the prescribed treatment regimen
4. The presence of Antisocial Personality Disorder.[82]

claim, or workers' compensation claim—there will always be a few people who will fake or exaggerate an injury or illness in order to cash in.

Factitious disorders, which *are* considered to be mental disorders in the *DSM–IV–TR*, also involve feigning, exaggerating, or self-inducing illness or injury. In the case of factitious disorders, however, the motivation for the behavior is not some external incentive, like avoiding responsibility or getting money, but rather a psychological need on the part of the individual to be a patient.

Disability Fraud: A Pathology or Just Going with the Flow?

In his book *Accidentally, on Purpose: The Making of a Personal Injury Underworld in America*, Ken Dornstein describes how faking accidents and illness—and sometimes injuring oneself or voluntarily being injured by another—has a long history in the United States. Some of the perpetrators of such frauds were legends in their time, at least among insurance adjusters, with many creative and notorious characters making this a career. In fact, a small percentage of people have always taken advantage of personal injury, disability, and workers' compensation systems. The more generous the compensation system, the more likely fraud was (and is).[83]

In October 2011, eleven people, including two doctors and a former union president, were indicted on charges of mail fraud and conspiracy to commit health care fraud for assisting hundreds of Long Island Rail Road workers in filing false disability pension claims. The cost of the allegedly false claims if they were all paid out? About $1 billion. As the *New York Times* had reported in a 2008 investigation, virtually every career employee of the Long Island Rail Road was retiring on a disability pension. According to the 2011 charges, the two doctors indicted, along with another doctor who died during the course of the investigation, were responsible for more than 75 percent of the false claims—documenting nonexistent or grossly exaggerated, allegedly job-related, employment-disabling physical impairments in individuals who went on to play golf and tennis multiple times a week, shovel snow, and go on long-distance bicycle rides.[84] The charges had not been resolved as of this publication, but they are certainly not the first or last of their kind.

Estimates of the prevalence of malingering and exaggeration vary. In a study published in 2002, psychology researchers at Nova Southeastern University in Florida surveyed members of the American Board of Clinical Neuropsychology—psychologists who assess impaired brain function—and concluded that malingering and exaggeration occurred in 29 percent of personal injury cases, 30 percent of disability cases, 19 percent of criminal cases, and 8 percent of medical cases.[85] Those are pretty high rates, but it is important to keep in mind that this is survey data, as opposed to a rigorous scientific study, and that it involves claims of cognitive impairment—which people often think is easier to fake than it really is. Similar results were found in a review of more objective studies of malingering, also in head injury cases.[86] And in chronic pain cases referred for psychological assessment, researchers at the University of New Orleans found that malingering occurred in 20 to 50 percent of cases where there was financial incentive to report illness or injury.[87] In another study of chronic-pain claims, psychologists concluded that the availability of compensation is related to how much pain people report experiencing and how effective their treatment is.[88] In other words, the availability of compensation for pain may provide an incentive to complain more about it and a disincentive to engage in treatment.

Does that make all those people who malinger or exaggerate their pain almost psychopaths? No. Many people who behave this way are either reacting in a normal psychological way to the possibility of receiving rewards for being ill or, as we suggested in the railroad disability cases, are responding in a very logical way to what the marketplace is offering them: "I used to work, then I got injured, and now my work is to be a patient, and that means I have to be sick." When the psychological and financial incentives for giving up the sick role outweigh the benefits of remaining ill or injured, many of these people will show improvement.

Before you look skeptically at any people you know who are receiving workers' compensation or disability payments, or who complain that they can't go to work because of, say, back pain, keep this in mind: these systems serve an important social function and abuses are the exception, not the rule. Although there is evidence that malingering and exaggeration of symptoms are real problems, they may occur less frequently than we might assume. Some of our perhaps exaggerated concern may be attributable to media coverage—scandals make the news, but there is little reporting of the countless times when the system functions properly and workers receive fair and appropriate compensation for very real injuries. Also, some data suggest that malingering may occur less frequently than we fear, with criminal fraud occurring in less than 2 percent of workplace compensation claims.[89]

What to Make of Our Two Disability Cases?

All people who consciously fake or self-induce injury are not the same; many almost certainly belong in at least our almost psychopath group. Let's consider our cases again.

Bob had no history of criminal or other antisocial behavior. He was a husband, father, and grandfather with no prior involvement in the legal system. A psychopath? It seems unlikely. But given the opportunity and the motivation to take financial advantage of the system, Bob and his wife, who was clearly an accomplice, decided to stage his illness. Perhaps he was just a primarily honest guy who, after a lifetime of hard work, couldn't handle it anymore and decided to take advantage of what was available to him. Not a psychopath, and maybe not even an almost psychopath—just a guy who slipped a bit on the moral standards and couldn't pass up a good thing, not unlike those who overestimate their in-kind donation to charity on their tax form or take those pens home from work.

Nevertheless, there were a few things that indicate that Bob belongs at least in the almost psychopath category. First, we should note the degree of planning in this case. Bob had purchased those other private disability policies two years earlier—unusual given his job, his overall good health, and the expense of the premiums compared to his income. For someone at his salary level, these policies represented a disproportionally large investment, unless there was an anticipation of future returns. And then there is the issue of the suspicious timing—the policies had a two-year waiting period before a claim could be filed under them. Finally, and more important, Bob and his wife also filed a personal injury suit against the auto service center accusing them of negligence for failing to tighten the lug nuts. The

213

service center fought the case and during the investigation found a witness who had seen Bob by the side of the road, just prior to the supposed accident, apparently loosening those same lug nuts. Bob withdrew that suit as well.

What about cases where there are widespread fraudulent disability claims, like the railroad example? For some claimants, scamming the disability system may be consistent with their behavior in the rest of their lives. Such people are true psychopaths or close to it. We suspect, however, that many, if not all, people who make fraudulent disability claims carry on the rest of their personal and business relationships in a basically legitimate way: fulfilling their obligations, caring for others, and staying out of trouble. But they may well belong to that group of otherwise law-abiding citizens who come to believe that exploitation of a system is just how it's done. And while these people would never steal from a neighbor or shoplift, they draw a distinction between wronging an individual and taking advantage of a nameless bureaucracy that they feel owes them something. Cheating the disability systems is viewed as a normal, moral behavior, just as fudging on income taxes is for others. It's just what's done.

In fact, retiring on a disability pension—even a fraudulent one—can be seen as an entitlement, something that workers count on in their financial planning. Such claimants may even have made their decisions about the houses and cars they own now and the schools their children attend based on their expectation of receiving retirement plus a disability pension—just like their colleagues who had retired before them. (As Milton Friedman pointed out in his theory of the permanent income hypothesis, which won him the Nobel Prize in economics,

people make current spending decisions based on their antici-
pated future earnings.)

So, in the minds of some people, filing a fraudulent disability claim is not stealing; it is part of the retirement planning
process. If I work for this company, I can expect to retire on
a disability pension, just like all those who came before me. All
I have to do is to go see a certain doctor and fill out the forms,
and it will come my way. The rationalizations that get them
by without the slightest twinge of guilt are easy: "Everyone
else has done it; I would be stupid not to. If it were so wrong,
why would it be allowed to go on? I worked hard for my entire
career and could have made more money elsewhere; this is
deferred compensation. The company/government has already
budgeted for this."

Almost Psychopaths and Unethical Decision Making

One response to stories of false disability claims, especially
when we hear of long-running, organized schemes, is to ask:
How can people feel okay with what they're doing? Generally,
these aren't career criminals. They're people who have (or
had) respectable jobs and careers, who support their families
and have standing in the community. And in many cases these
aren't spur-of-the-moment decisions born of sudden dire
circumstances. Many involved in such schemes consciously,
deliberately, and over an extended period of time engage in
what they know is fraud.

Unethical behavior isn't limited to doctors and the people
who make illegitimate disability claims. The news is filled
with stories of unprincipled behavior in the corporate and
professional worlds. Whether it's a chief financial officer

intentionally misleading regulators and investors about the financial condition of a company or a lawyer pilfering the trust account of her incapacitated client or police officers fixing tickets for their family and friends, we are constantly reminded that some people blithely disregard the law. And at times, it is the same law that they have sworn to uphold.

As we've discussed, conning and deception are markers of psychopathy. It's easy to see how true psychopaths could lie in an accounting statement, falsify a medical claim, or steal from a client, but unless they are extremely skilled, they won't be able to get away with it over the long term. It is the almost psychopath who is more likely to succeed at flying below the radar and gaining a position of authority in a business or profession.

The problem with almost psychopaths at work may extend beyond what is plainly illegal behavior (stealing company property, filing fraudulent disability claims) to unethical conduct in more ambiguous situations. A recent study published in the *Journal of Business Ethics* suggests that almost psychopaths are more likely to make unethical decisions about moral dilemmas and that one way to explain this is the process of *moral disengagement.*[90] This idea arises from a theory of social cognition that says people judge their actions by comparing them to a set of internal moral standards. The thought is that this internal supervisory mechanism can be switched on or off, and that moral disengagement is a person's ability to unhitch, or disengage, his or her actions from moral standards by justifying them in various ways that allow the behavior without causing distress. The justifications can focus on the behavior itself, for example, by comparing it to actions that could be worse or using euphemisms to make the action seem less negative.

They can focus on the person himself or herself, by assigning responsibility for the overall situation to someone else in the organization, for example. Or the rationalization can turn to the victims of the unethical behavior, by holding that they somehow "deserve" to be treated in this way. All of this comes under the umbrella of "self-serving cognitive distortions" that we mentioned earlier.

The researchers collected data from 272 undergraduate students at a large university who received course credit for their participation. The students were asked to complete a psychopathy scale assessment (the Self-Report Psychopathy Scale). They were also given four scenarios with different ethical predicaments that might arise in the business world (for example, disclosing errors in a financial statement or taking shortcuts in order to meet a production schedule) and an unethical response to each. They were then asked to rate their approval of eight separate justifications—all associated with moral disengagement—on a scale of 1 ("strongly agree") to 7 ("strongly disagree"). The results showed that those students with psychopathic tendencies were more likely to respond unethically to dilemmas in a business setting than the general population and that moral disengagement is one explanation for this tendency.

The Con Artist

The term *con* comes from the word *confidence* and refers to the fact that in order to fool people into doing what they want, con men and women first earn the confidence of their victims. These characters are the stuff of legends, from the salesperson who offers you, and only you, the deal of a lifetime, to the guy who runs the game of three-card monte on the street corner, to Ponzi and his famous scheme (not to mention his modern-day heir—Bernie Madoff). And let's not forget Frank Abagnale. Who? Abagnale was a "paper hanger"—passing bad checks reportedly worth $2.5 million, then traveling around the world as a guest of other airlines by masquerading as an airline pilot, and subsequently working as a doctor and then a lawyer. He was eventually imprisoned in France, then in the United States, but he escaped from a federal penitentiary by posing as a Bureau of Prisons undercover agent. Recaptured and imprisoned, he earned an early release by agreeing to donate his time helping the federal government fight fraud. He now runs a financial fraud consulting firm.

"The con" is a source of wonder and even entertainment—as long as you are not the victim! Abagnale was the subject of the 2002 film *Catch Me if You Can* starring Leonardo DiCaprio and Tom Hanks. The 1988 film *Dirty Rotten Scoundrels*, starring Michael Caine, Steve Martin, and Glenne Headly, is an amusing story of two con men who are ultimately outconned themselves. Plenty of laughs and a degree of satisfaction there, as the only people being duped are the con artists. But in real life, the cons are far more painful and damaging, and much less amusing.

Connie and her accomplice husband are examples of low-level, but unfortunately fairly common, con artists. She literally tried to "cash in" on the trust and affection she'd help develop. Are Connie and her husband psychopaths? Almost. How close they come to ratings as true psychopaths on the PCL–R will depend on such factors as whether they moved to the community with the intention of carrying out this scam and if they had run it somewhere else before. There might be some mitigating factors that lead us to grade them less harshly, but claiming to have cancer, continuing to lie about it, and working on a tan while telling people you are getting chemotherapy puts them at least into the almost category.

Munchausen Syndrome

Where does Sally stand in all of this? Sally suffers from Munchausen syndrome, a factitious disorder that is very much on Axis I of the *DSM–IV–TR*. Rather than pursuing financial gain or other benefit, she is putting her health at risk to satisfy some deep psychological need. Munchausen syndrome is among the oddest and most perplexing disorders that medical professionals encounter. It is difficult for anyone, including physicians, to understand why someone would willfully under-go invasive medical tests, confine themselves to a hospital, manipulate their vital signs or laboratory tests, or even injure themselves. It is estimated that two-thirds of patients with Munchausen work in the medical field in some way, and the majority are men who are relatively socially isolated. While another Axis I mental illness, such as depression, can be at play in some of these cases, the majority of people with Munchausen syndrome have some sort of personality disturbance, such as borderline or histrionic personality disorder.[91] In the absence of other factors, they are not likely to fall into the almost psychopath range.

Most clinicians believe that the underlying motivation for faking an illness is to assume the sick role, be cared for, and get attention from medical professionals. In the quest for this attention and caring, these patients actually end up alienating and angering the very professionals with whom they seek to be close. Clinicians feel cheated and duped when they learn that their time and good-faith efforts to help a patient have been expended on someone whose illness is self-induced. As the medical community has come to learn that there is a difference between willful malingering for personal gain (such as feigning pain to obtain narcotics) and conditions like Munchausen syndrome, the disorder has generated less hostility and more clinical concern. Rather than feeling that they have been duped by an almost psychopath or psychopath, clinicians recognize that this behavior is the result of a mental disorder connected with a very real and deep psychological disturbance.

Typically, patients with Munchausen syndrome deny inducing their illness when confronted about their behavior, and if the issue is pressed, they will sign out of the hospital or leave their treating physician. The classic Munchausen syndrome patient is thought to travel from city to city, pursuing medical attention in a way that makes it difficult for the behavior to be tracked. Discovery of their patterns generally requires a fair amount of medical detective work, and most physicians and medical facilities do not have time, especially in this modern era of shortened appointments and hospital stays. It will be interesting to see what the advent of electronic medical records, as well as personalized medical records that patients can carry with them, has on Munchausen syndrome.

Clinicians have a harder time coming to grips with a related condition that is even more disturbing: Munchausen syndrome by proxy. In this disorder, a parent or other adult responsible for a child claims that the child is ill or actually induces illness

SICK OR SLICK? ❖

in the child. The most notorious of cases involve causing infections, contaminating laboratory samples, and causing the child to have to undergo invasive procedures, or smothering the child in an effort to simulate a respiratory arrest.

Why would anyone do such a thing? Theories include a desire to gain attention from the medical profession or to be seen as a devoted and caring parent. The person with Munchausen syndrome by proxy is usually, but not always, a mother and may have a history of child abuse or neglect or early loss of a parent. Detection of these cases often requires video surveillance in an inpatient setting. As this disorder has become better known, it has unfortunately also given rise to false accusations, including in child custody cases where one parent accuses the other of Munchausen by proxy.

What to Do?

Most of us are not responsible for the problem of fighting disability fraud, although we all pay the price through higher premiums and a more difficult claims process in which everyone's claim for benefits is regarded as suspect. In general, we are hesitant to speak up if someone seems to be scamming the system, probably due to a combination of a general "mind my own business" viewpoint, preference not to get involved, and fear of being wrong. Whistle-blower statutes, which offer protection and financial rewards to people whose reports of fraud and abuse lead to convictions, have helped reduce some of this reluctance.

Many would do well to consider how we can avoid being scammed by con artists. Connie, after all, was not some slick outsider who rolled into town selling something. (Remember

Professor Harold Hill in *The Music Man?*) She was the beloved town crossing guard! Protection lies in combining one's generosity of spirit and empathy with a healthy skepticism. Most of us find it hard to believe that someone we even know, let alone care about, is capable of a criminal act like this. But there is an endless supply of examples where the family, friends, and colleagues of a perpetrator have had to come to grips with the guilt of the person we defended so adamantly. (Of course, in some cases the denial runs so deep that they never accept the facts and remain at risk of being duped again.)

When it comes to charities of any type, it is important to ask questions. An online search will turn up any number of fraudulent fund-raising schemes. Before you give money to any fund-raising effort, check it out. The Internet is a wonderful tool for discovering which "charities" are frauds and which are legitimate. When it comes to a local charitable event, like raising money for Connie, don't be afraid to ask questions. As we have said elsewhere, trust your instincts and check them out with others. You may just find that others share your doubts about how someone so sick can look so good. But besides providing a way to check out potential scams, the Internet has also opened up new opportunities for fraudsters and con artists. (Is there anyone who hasn't received an e-mail from the former African princess/oil minister/bank executive who will cut you in on millions of dollars if you send some good-faith money and your bank account information?)

Finally, what about Munchausen syndrome? You can look for the same clues that we do in medicine: someone who insists on lots of attention for his or her medical condition, works in the medical field, frequently changes caregivers, seeks treatment in far-flung places, and provides a vague history of multiple complaints. Such a patient may be exhibiting Munchausen syndrome. This syndrome is relatively rare, but other disorders, such as hypochondria (a tendency to be overly concerned about minor physical problems), are much more common. Patients with Munchausen syndrome require a great deal of support and encouragement to engage in psychotherapy. The same is true of those with hypochondriasis, who may also be suffering from a more treatable anxiety or mood disorder.

If you suspect that someone suffers from Munchausen syndrome by proxy, it is important that you document your concerns, discuss them with a medical professional, and then, if necessary, report them to the appropriate social service agency. A child's life may be at stake, and it is better to risk being wrong than to risk having to bear the burden of not getting involved in what might very well lead to a tragic outcome.

| 11 |

What to Do When You Find Yourself in Almost Psychopath Territory

We have filled this book with multiple examples of terrible behavior and its consequences—something of a rogue's gallery that ranges from people who strayed off their normal path to almost psychopaths and on up to the PCL–R-certifiable, full-blown psychopath. In presenting these cases, we couldn't possibly cover every scenario in which you might encounter an almost psychopath, but we hope that we have made you aware that an almost psychopath *could* be lurking in any corner of your life. We didn't do this to shock or to titillate, but to simply inform you that these things happen to real people and they are done by real people. And now it is time to review what can and, in some cases, cannot be done to help you deal with an almost psychopath or with similar traits if you find them in yourself.

Speaking Up and the Decision to Act

The realization that someone might be an almost psychopath (or full-blown psychopath) probably won't come out of the blue like a bolt of lightning. It sneaks up on you, one odd experience, betrayal, or deception at a time. It's like the old story about the frog in the pot: if you place a frog in a pot of cold water on the stove and the heat is turned up gradually, the frog will stay put until you've made frog soup. But if that same frog is thrown into a pot of hot water on the stove, it will jump out immediately. (Or so we're told; we actually haven't tried it—nor do we plan to.)

So what does this story have to do with you and the almost psychopaths? Just this: the clues revealing that you are dealing with an almost or true psychopath may be subtle and accumulate over time. Many people feel ashamed and are angry with themselves when their 20/20 hindsight kicks in and they realize they have been duped or otherwise victimized by someone like this. But there is no shame in it. As we noted with regard to Greta (our example of the almost psychopath in the workplace), Ron often reminds his trainees that these folks are far better at what they do than we will ever be at detecting their devious ways in advance or as they are manipulating us. They get as far as they do because they are smooth and skilled and take advantage of the better natures of those around them.

To protect yourself, use your situational awareness: live your life but pay attention to your feelings, to the people around you, and to the events in your life—especially if they are unusual. Think critically about events and behaviors that affect you. Does that other person in your life make you feel anxious, demeaned, or used? Do you find yourself confused as you deal with this person, either in terms of your feelings or in terms of facts? Are you made to feel unsure of what you've seen or heard—*gaslighted*, so to speak? (You may be familiar with this term, a reference to the 1944 film *Gaslight* and the play by the same name. It tells the story of a woman whose new husband attempts to trick her into believing that she is insane by manipulating their environment and causing her to doubt her own perceptions—what has come to be referred to as *gaslighting*.) Pay attention to the behaviors and symptoms that you now know are associated with psychopathy: the odd experiences, betrayals, deceptions, examples of callous behaviors toward you and others, the lack of responsibility or remorse, and the rest.

Let's say that over time you suspect you are involved with an almost psychopath or true psychopath—at home, work, or elsewhere. You start to get the sense that you are in the pot and it is definitely getting warmer, but you don't know for sure, and you certainly don't want to make a mistake—by over- or under-reacting. Keep these considerations and actions in mind:

1. To address the problem, you first have to be willing to accept the possibility that you are in a very bad situation, perhaps with someone to whom you are closely attached. Accept the fact that this can and does happen. Willingness to acknowledge that a problem exists is the first step in recovering from all sorts of problems, including bad relationships, and in preventing further harm.

2. Believe that you are not helpless: you can do something about this. You may not be able to solve the problem instantly or even in the short term, but there is hope.

3. Document, privately and carefully, the behaviors and

events that concern you. Review them periodically. Do you see a pattern? Have things escalated or improved? Are you the frog in the pot, slowly getting cooked, because your tolerance and good nature allowed you to overlook just how bad things have become?

4. Reach out for help to friends, family members, and professionals. Trust your gut instincts, and if your concerns are rejected, look to someone else for support.

5. Be willing to say something. The silence of those who psychopaths and almost psychopaths betray, manipulate, and abuse is perhaps the greatest ally they possess. It was a few brave individuals, those willing to speak up and face public and professional resistance, who overcame individual and institutional disbelief and began the movements to address domestic violence, sexual misconduct by priests and therapists, and child sexual abuse.

6. If you find yourself being hurt or otherwise abused, get out as quickly and safely as you can. No one has the right to physically, verbally, or emotionally hurt another person. And you do not deserve to be treated that way.

A word of warning: while it is important to trust your perceptions and concerns, try to remain open to the possibility that you may be misperceiving events or that the problems are transitory or have other explanations. One of our favorite movies, *Rashomon*, examines the complexity of perception. The 1950 film by the famed Japanese director Akira Kurosawa presents the story of a violent crime recounted by four witnesses, including the perpetrator and the victims, who give similar but ultimately contradictory versions of the same event.

Kurosawa was ahead of his time, anticipating the now well-established doubtful reliability of eyewitness testimony and the subjective way in which we all view the world.

If confronted on their behavior, almost or true psychopaths will often use their ability to charm and deceive to convince mutual friends, family, and therapists that you are wrong about things and that *you* are the unreasonable one, as evidenced by your refusal to even consider other possibilities. It is important that you be the one who is calm, rational, and steady in how you address the problem and demonstrate your ability to assess the situation objectively.

What if you are the frog plunked into hot water: you suddenly find yourself thrown into a situation in which you or those you care about are being betrayed, cheated, abused, manipulated, or generally victimized? The same considerations apply. Get out of the situation as quickly and safely as possible. Different circumstances will call for different strategies, but always document your concerns and keep track of them. Push through any embarrassment you might feel about having gotten into such a difficult situation and ask for help from those who can provide it. Talking to friends and professionals about relationship issues, seeking the help of victim advocates in cases of domestic abuse, making use of the available complaint and investigatory mechanisms in the workplace, and turning to law enforcement and social service agencies when you or your children are at risk are all appropriate actions. Remind yourself of the risks of not acting. Have the courage to take that step and speak up. Public attitudes regarding abusive relationships may not be perfect, and neither are many institutional policies and practices. But many have improved the way they screen and monitor individuals who have the responsibility and privilege of caring for, protecting, teaching, and coaching others. This process will continue to improve in society only if victims are willing to come forward and receive the support they need and deserve.

What if, quite to your surprise, you learn or believe that someone you trust and feel close to has committed a terrible act? The decision to report your concerns or knowledge is one of the most daunting people face. The more we know (or believe we know) the person accused, the more difficult it is to accept that he or she did something improper, especially something that seriously harms a child or other innocent victim. If the evidence is at all ambiguous, we likely err on the side of keeping quiet, for fear of being wrong and embarrassing a "good" person and ourselves.

Terrible damage to individuals and institutions can occur when we don't take personal responsibility for preventing and responding to potentially psychopathic and illicit behavior. As we sat down to write this last chapter, the Penn State University football scandal broke. Former Penn State assistant football coach Jerry Sandusky was indicted on charges that, for over a decade, he had sexually abused boys who were receiving services from a foundation for troubled youth that he had established. The allegations severely damaged the reputation of the program and school, resulted in charges against university officials, and brought to a crashing end the storied career of the late head coach Joe Paterno. As of this writing, it is a tragic story of both individual and institutional failure to accept and respond to accusations of horrendous behavior by a supposedly well-liked and respected individual.

It is not difficult to find other examples of institutions that ignored, denied, minimized, rationalized, and just plain mishandled allegations of serious misconduct by their members. The Catholic Church's response to allegations that priests sexually abused children is a prime example, as is the way in which the psychoanalytic institutes and the rest of the mental health community responded (or did not respond) to reports of therapists being sexually involved with their patients.

The decision to take action is almost always difficult. It is easiest when we are acting to protect someone else and when our emotional and institutional ties to the accused are weak. It is more difficult when we are acting to protect ourselves, often because we fear that we are acting out of petty self-interest or doubt our facts and perceptions, fear being wrong, or cannot bring ourselves to make accusations against an institution that others love and respect. In addition, when we make allegations of wrongdoing against the institution and individuals within it who are respected and liked, we dread bringing attention to ourselves as accusers and being ostracized by the community. These feelings are well grounded.

There *are* risks to speaking up and breaking through the individual and institutional denial that something is wrong. It's hard to overcome a desire to avoid controversy. Whether it is a question of challenging the manipulative behavior of the bullying co-worker, the con artist, the abusive partner, or the sexually abusive doctor, therapist, or coach, taking action requires courage. If you can acknowledge that bad things can and do happen and that you can do something to avert further harm to yourself or others, courage may be easier to find. In such situations, it is worth remembering a quote attributed to the ancient Jewish scholar Rabbi Hillel: "If I am not for myself, then who will be for me? And if I am only for myself, then what am I? And if not now, when?" Often copied and repeated, this quote has been shortened in modern times to an even more direct encouragement to individual responsibility in response to threats to communities and individuals: "If not me, who? If not now, when?"

Treatment and Trying to Make Things Right

To reach the point where you decide to act, you may well need some help and support as you weigh the pros and cons, and address some of your own psychological issues. The best place to start is with friends and family members, but that is not always possible (after all, they may be the problem) and you may not always find a receptive audience, as some of our case examples have shown. If turning to family and friends is not an option for you, consider consulting with a psychiatrist, psychologist, or social worker. We're talking about a specific consultation in which you talk about the situation with the goal of getting a handle on the problem, your options, and the pros and cons of taking certain steps. We encourage you, if possible, to find someone who has experience with the particular problem you are facing, whether it is conflict in your relationship with a loved one, concerns about your child or adolescent, conflicts at work, or concerns about possible sexual misconduct. There are lots of mental health professionals out there, and they are not all equal in terms of expertise, knowledge, training, or skill. Shop for the help you need. You are the customer and deserve to get the right help from the right person.

We recommend asking for referrals from your local hospitals, academic medical centers, professional organizations, or friends who are familiar with the field, rather than looking for names on the Internet. Remember, anyone can post anything on the Web, and even sites that claim to rate practitioners often have ratings from a just a handful of people who are not necessarily objective in their assessments. If it is the practitioner's own website that contains the accolades, be skeptical—no one is going to post bad reviews of themselves.

Confronting Problem Behavior

Let's say you have gathered your courage and decided something needs to be done. It is possible to work constructively with the almost psychopath in your life. Here are some suggestions:

Speak up. Address your concerns with the person in question, if it is possible to do so safely from a physical, emotional, and professional standpoint. Many people are truly unaware of their own behavior, which they may view as benign while you experience it as completely malignant. Pay attention to how the people you confront listen to you and how they respond. Do they launch into defensive mode and flatly deny your concerns, minimize them, or blame them on you? If so, that's a bad sign. On the other hand, you can be more optimistic if they listen and actively attempt to understand your perspective, even if they don't completely share it. The goal is to problem-solve the situation with this person and to have a real conversation. A conversation, even about heated and contentious issues, is an exchange of viewpoints and information, not a diatribe in which one person vents and the other listens and has to yield at the end.

Proceed with patience. Keep in mind that the problem does not have to be solved in one sitting. Once energized to address a problem, some people go after it like a dog with a bone: they sink their teeth into it and won't let go until it has been resolved to their satisfaction—definitely not a conversational or problem-solving approach. In this counterproductive scenario, any attempt by the other party to take a break from the discussion or slow things down is interpreted as avoidance or a sign of weakness. With that attitude, the initiator may turn the "conversation" into even more of an attack, leading the other person to become defensive and angry. What was intended to be a discussion between two people to resolve a problem in their relationship blows up into an argument or ends up as passive submission that satisfies one and leaves the other resentful. The more productive approach is truly conversational in nature, with the initiating party clearly stating his or her concerns and sincerely looking to understand the other person's perspective. That signals interest in the other person's opinion, as well as respect, rather than an attack on their character, even while stating a grievance.

Track progress. Okay, you've gotten this far. You have raised your concerns and addressed the issues, and both parties have emerged with little more than ruffled feathers and perhaps with expressions of respect and appreciation for one another. You may have gotten responses that range from "I'm sorry; it won't happen again" to expression of what appears to be genuine understanding. What happens next? Now is the time to see if the behavior changes, both in the short and the long term. Old habits are hard to break and personalities endure over time, so just as the issue won't necessarily be resolved in one sitting, we can't expect behavior to suddenly and permanently change after one conversation. The concerns may have to be raised again, but hopefully the next time(s) doing so will be easier. Pay attention, though, to repeated incidents. Signs that there has not been a meeting of the minds and that your concerns have not been heard include automatic apologies, dismissive comments about your concerns, and passive-aggressive behavior in which the other person acts out his or her irritation with the complaints in other areas, such as when a spouse or partner fails to perform household chores after a discussion about spending too much money.

Seek additional help. Suppose you've talked to the person about the problem, but it has not completely resolved or there are ongoing feelings of frustration and dissatisfaction. If this is happening within a romantic relationship, it's time to consider some type of clinical intervention. Couples therapy can help people address these relationship problems, although too often the couple enters therapy much too late to have any hope of salvaging the relationship. The refusal of one partner to agree to the other's sincere request to "see somebody" together is a bad sign. Sure, many people are skeptical of mental health professionals and psychotherapy, but in this context, the refusal to even try therapy usually reflects denial that they have any role in the difficulty, disbelief that they have any problems of their own, or fear of addressing what problems they do have. It is possible that the individual would be willing to go into treatment on his or her own, but in our experience, it's not highly likely. (As we noted earlier, the higher up on the psychopathy scale a person is, the less successful treatment is.) If your spouse or partner refuses counseling, you should consider individual treatment for yourself to gain perspective on your feelings and to consider how you might want to move forward.

Find help at the workplace. If the person you're concerned about is someone in your workplace or other professional or community setting, and you have failed to make progress by dealing with him or her directly, bump the problem up to the next higher level of authority. Talk to your supervisors or other authorities about the problem. While no one is going to suggest couples therapy, someone may suggest team-building exercises at work or a community meeting to talk about the situation. Take advantage of these opportunities and try to do so with an open mind, as they may lead to at least partial resolution and will show that you are a reasonable person trying to solve a problem. While you are pursuing these options, stay attuned to whether the other person's actions match his or her words.

If all else fails. What if none of these efforts work after a new problem arises or after years of difficulties? Your choices are to turn down the heat on the pot (an option that the poor frogs don't have) or jump out. Individual or couples therapy may be a way to turn down the heat, but it is not always successful. In fact, entering therapy after years of difficulty may help a person finally realize that he or she has been cooking for a long time, and it is time to jump. If you decide it is time to jump, try to find a neutral person who can hear you out and respond objectively. A good therapist will not tell you what to do but will help guide you through the various considerations as you make up your own mind.

What If Your Own Behavior Is the Problem?

Most of this book has discussed psychopathic traits in other people and what to do when you discover them. Let's give a bit more attention to what you can do if you are concerned about your own behavior.

As we noted earlier, the fact that you are concerned is a positive sign from the standpoint of whether you belong on the almost psychopath spectrum. It is an even more positive sign that you have the insight to recognize a possible problem with your interactions with others and your own responsibility for addressing it. And even if you do earn a few more points on the various PCL scales than one would like, hope is not lost. Forget the label: you have already learned something about yourself, even if you don't like it, and you may be ready to act.

Just as when you're reacting to the problem behavior of others, you can follow some key steps in taking action about your own behavior:

1. Acknowledge that there is a problem, even if you can't quite put your finger on what it is. This may be the hardest part, because it requires accepting that you may be the primary, or at least a significant, part of the difficulties in your own life. Your problems may even be among the more serious and disturbing we've discussed in our case examples: intimate partner violence, sexual attraction to children, bullying behavior, or criminal acts. Or, when considered objectively, you may be worried about relatively minor problems. At this point, you probably don't have a very clear sense of what the problem is, and in fact, you may be overestimating its significance. Approach this as a chance to learn more about yourself, rather than as a trip to the proverbial woodshed to be punished for being a bad person.

2. Ask for help—from friends, family, and colleagues. You'll be amazed at how well people respond to requests for help, especially from those who are sincerely looking for ways to improve their lives and the lives of those around them. Most societies and cultures have a soft spot for those who seek to make up for their missteps and turn their lives around. Americans, in particular, are usually open to forgiving and accepting even those people whose misdeeds have been on public display in a very public fashion. Eliot Spitzer—the disgraced former governor of New York who resigned in the midst of a sensational prostitution scandal—hosted a television news program for a time after his resignation and has since been considered a possible mayoral candidate for the city of New York. Even former president Richard Nixon was rehabilitated toward the end of his life, with people remembering the positive things he accomplished, though not entirely forgetting the negatives.

3. Family, friends, and colleagues can only do so much, and you should seriously consider seeking help from a therapist who has expertise in working with personality disorders and relationship problems.

4. Ask for forgiveness for what you have done that hurt others. No illusions here: there are some acts from which people cannot recover, but these tend to involve the extremes of psychopathic behavior. If you are in the almost range, there may still be hope of rebuilding some, if not all, of the bridges you burned along the way.

Forgiveness: Responding to the Almost Psychopath in Our Lives and Ourselves

What if someone in your life has disappointed, hurt, or betrayed you in a way that made you reach for this book? Or what if you were the one who committed the offensive acts? Human error and frailty, and the regularity with which one person harms or offends another, are common themes in the world's religions. Even the case studies we've included in our book illustrate the extent to which even normally upright people are prone to doing bad things at times. Judaism, Christianity, Islam, Buddhism, and Hinduism all teach the importance of seeking and granting forgiveness. Over the last several decades, researchers have shown that individuals who can forgive those who have harmed or offended them are psychologically and physically healthier, not to mention happier.[92]

Perhaps one of the greatest distinctions between an almost psychopath and a true psychopath is in the ability to seek and grant forgiveness. Those who have offended or harmed others but who can acknowledge and appreciate the hurt they have caused—showing true empathy—don't belong in either of those categories. Their sense that they need to genuinely apologize and their desire to be forgiven are good signs—they show that, no matter the transgression, the essential elements of psychopathy are absent. However, if you are the one asking for forgiveness, don't count on getting it, especially if your actions were extremely hurtful and damaging. If you are forgiven, it may mark the start of repairing, at least to some extent, any harm you have caused. The key factor in seeking forgiveness, regardless of whether you receive it, is that you have come clean with yourself. You can now move ahead, we hope, having learned how to avoid similar missteps in the future.

And what about offering forgiveness? That's a bit more complicated. Almost psychopaths, feeling no empathy and being totally focused on themselves, are unlikely to be able to forgive even someone who is asking for forgiveness. And they may well go beyond that, looking to exact revenge. On the other hand, sometimes individuals cannot offer forgiveness, even when it is sincerely sought, because of the nature of the transgression and their own psychological makeup—not necessarily because they are almost psychopaths. Psychotherapy can be helpful in getting you to the point where you can offer forgiveness or at least understand why you simply cannot.

In helping you identify situations where you might be dealing with almost psychopaths, we are encouraging you to take the steps necessary to protect yourself and those around you, or to change your own behavior if you feel you are the one with the problem. And we certainly want you to believe that you have both the right and the obligation to act in these situations. But we are also encouraging you to leave the door open to the possibility that people can change and to the hope that those who are somewhere along the almost psychopath continuum can reverse their direction and come to live in society with no more than the usual array of flaws that we all share. Protecting yourself and your loved ones, while at the same time holding on to a well-grounded hope for better things, is difficult to do. But it's well worth it.

■ ◆ ■

appendix A

Diagnostic Criteria
for Antisocial Personality Disorder

A. There is a pervasive pattern of disregard for and violation of the rights of others occurring since the age of 15 years, as indicated by three (or more) of the following:

1. Failure to conform to social norms with respect to lawful behaviors, as indicated by repeatedly performing acts that are grounds for arrest;

2. Deceitfulness, as indicated by repeated lying, use of aliases, or conning others for personal profit or pleasure;

3. Impulsivity or failure to plan ahead;

4. Irritability and aggressiveness, as indicated by repeated physical fights or assaults;

5. Reckless disregard for safety of self or others;

6. Consistent irresponsibility, as indicated by repeated failure to sustain consistent work behavior or honor financial obligations; and

7. Lack of remorse, as indicated by being indifferent to or rationalizing having hurt, mistreated, or stolen from another.

B. The individual is at least age 18 years.

C. There is evidence of Conduct Disorder with onset before age 15 years.

D. The occurrence of antisocial behavior is not exclusively during the course of Schizophrenia or a Manic Episode.

Source: American Psychiatric Association, *Diagnostic and Statistical Manual of Mental Disorders*, 4th ed., text rev. (Washington, DC: American Psychiatric Association, 2000), Criteria 301.7, page 706.

• • •

Authors' note: The fifth edition of the *DSM* is expected to take a dimensional, instead of a categorical, approach to mental disorders. That is, rather than requiring a determination of whether an individual has or does not have a specific personality disorder, the approach allows consideration of the unique combination of different personality traits that contribute to a personality disorder diagnosis. The fifth edition will be published in 2013.

appendix B

Defining a Mental Disorder

Using the Axes of the *Diagnostic and Statistical Manual of Mental Disorders (DSM–IV–TR)*

The *DSM–IV–TR* provides a mechanism to define a given person's mental disorder along five "axes," similar to a graph's "x" and "y" axes. In addition, each disorder is assigned a code number that can be followed by additional numbers that add more detail about the diagnosis in that particular person.

Axis I is for what are commonly thought of as major mental disorders: major depression, bipolar disorder, psychotic disorders like schizophrenia, and anxiety disorders like panic disorder and post-traumatic stress disorder. Axis I also encompasses conditions that usually present in childhood (such as ADHD and autism), as well as substance abuse disorders, dementias, and other disorders resulting from medical conditions or exposure to toxins. Finally, Axis I includes conditions that are assigned to the category "V" codes—conditions that are not considered mental disorders but may be the subject of clinical attention.

These include malingering, problems in relationships, academic problems, occupational problems, adult and childhood antisocial behavior, and noncompliance with treatment.

Axis II includes personality disorders and developmental disorders like mental retardation. Personality traits—those psychological characteristics that make us individuals—are also coded on Axis II if they are contributing to distress or affecting functioning. Only problematic or negative traits are listed, and it's important to note that personality traits can be exacerbated during times of stress.

Axis III is for medical conditions that have an impact on the patient's mental health.

Axis IV includes problems generally regarded as life stressors. These can include

- Problems with relationships, owing to, for instance, separation or death of a family member, abuse, or conflict;
- Problems related to social support or living environment;
- Academic or learning problems;
- Workplace problems;
- Economic or housing problems;
- Legal problems; and
- Exposure to violence or inadequate health care.

Axis V is for what is called a Global Assessment of Functioning (GAF). GAF is used to estimate the patient's level of symptoms, impairment, or disability. For a collection of symptoms to be classified a "mental disorder" in the *DSM*, it must cause significant impairment in the ability to engage in life activities or cause significant emotional distress to the person with the symptoms.

For a full description of the axes, see the *Diagnostic and Statistical Manual of Mental Disorders*, 4th ed., text rev. (Washington, DC: American Psychiatric Association, 2000).

notes

Chapter 1: Setting the Stage

1. C. G. Jung, "Psychology and Religion," in *Psychology and Religion: West and East* (London: Routledge & Kegan Paul, 1958), 131.

2. A. M. Johnson, "Sanctions for Superego Lacunae of Adolescents," in *Searchlights on Delinquency*, ed. K. Eissler (New York: International Universities Press, 1949), 222–45.

3. D. DeSteno and P. Valdesolo, *Out of Character* (New York: Crown Archetype, 2011).

4. A. Guggenbühl-Craig, *The Emptied Soul: On the Nature of Psychopathy* (Putnam, CT: Spring Publications, 1980).

5. R. T. Salekin, "Treatment of Psychopathy: A Review and Brief Introduction to the Mental Model Approach for Psychopathy," *Behavioral Sciences and the Law* 28, no. 2 (2010): 235–66.

6. B. W. Dunlop, J. A. DeFife, L. Marx, S. J. Garlow, C. B. Nemeroff, and S.O. Lilienfeld, "The Effects of Sertraline on Psychopathic Traits," *International Clinical Psychopharmacology* 26, no. 6 (2011): 329–37.

Chapter 2: What Is a Psychopath?

7. E. Viding, R. J. R. Blair, T. Moffitt, and R. Plomin, "Evidence for Substantial Genetic Risk for Psychopathy in 7-Year-Olds," *Journal of Child Psychology and Psychiatry* 46.6 (2005): 592–97; M. Brook, M. S. Panizzon, D. S. Kosson, E. A. Sullivan, M. J. Lyons, C. E. Franz, S. A. Eisen, and W. S. Kremen, "Psychopathic Personality Traits in Middle-Aged Male Twins: A Behavior Genetic Investigation," *Journal of Personality Disorders* 24, no. 4 (2010): 473–86.

8. K. A. Kiehl, A. M. Smith, R. D. Hare, A. Mendrek, B. B. Forster, J. Brink, and P. F. Liddle, "Limbic Abnormalities in Affective Processing Criminal Psychopaths as Revealed by Functional Magnetic Resonance Imaging," *Biological Psychiatry* 50, no. 9 (2001): 677–82.

9. R. J. R. Blair, "Responding to the Emotions of Others: Dissociating Forms of Empathy through the Study of Typical and Psychiatric Populations," *Consciousness and Cognition* 14, no. 4 (2005): 698–718.

10. Q. Deeley, E. Daly, S. Surguladze, N. Tunstall, G. Mezey, D. Beer, A. Ambikapathy, D. Robertson, V. Giampietro, M. J. Brammer, A. Clarke, J. Dowsett, T. Fahy, M. L. Phillips, and D. G. Murphy, "Facial Emotion Processing in Criminal Psychopathy: Preliminary Functional Magnetic Imaging Study," *British Journal of Psychiatry* 189 (2006): 533–39.

11. H. Eisenbarth, G. W. Alpers, D. Segrè, A. Calogero, and A. Angrilli, "Categorization and Evaluation of Emotional Faces in Psychopathic Women," *Psychiatry Research* 159 (2008), 189–95.

12. J. Buckholtz, M. Treadway, R. Cowan, N. Woodward, S. Benning, R. Li, M. S. Ansari, R. Baldwin, A. Schwartzman, E. Shelby, C. Smith, D. Cole, R. Kessler, and D. Zald, "Mesolimbic Dopamine Reward System Hypersensitivity in Individuals with Psychopathic Traits," *Nature Neuroscience* 13, no. 3 (2010): 419–21.

13. Y. Yang, A. Raine, P. Colletti, A. W. Toga, and K. L. Narr, "Morphological Alterations in the Prefrontal Cortex and the Amygdala in Unsuccessful Psychopaths," *Journal of Abnormal Psychology* 119, no. 4 (2010): 863–74.

14. D. L. Paulus and K. M. Williams, "The Dark Triad of Personality: Narcissism, Machiavellianism, and Psychopathy," *Journal of Research in Personality* 36 (2002): 556–63.

15. T. L. Nicholls, J. R. P. Ogloff, J. Brink, and A. Spidel, "Psychopathy in Women: A Review of Its Clinical Usefulness for Assessing Risk for Aggression and Criminality," *Behavioral Sciences and the Law* 23, no. 6 (2005): 779–802.

16. R. D. Hare, C. Strachan, and A. E. Forth, "Psychopathy and Crime: An Overview," in *Clinical Approaches to the Mentally Disordered Offender*, eds. C. R. Hollin and K. Howells (Chichester, England: Wiley, 1993), 165–78.

17. S. Porter, A. R. Birt, and D. P. Boer, "Investigation of the Criminal and Conditional Release Profiles of Canadian Federal Offenders as a Function of Psychopathy and Age," *Law and Human Behavior* 25, no. 6 (2001): 647–61; S. Porter, M. Woodworth, J. Earle, J. Drugge, and D. Boer, "Characteristics of Sexual Homicides Committed by Psychopathic and Nonpsychopathic Offenders," *Law and Human Behavior* 27, no. 5 (2003): 459–70.

18. M. Woodworth and S. Porter, "In Cold Blood: Characteristics of Criminal Homicides as a Function of Psychopathy," *Journal of Abnormal Psychology* 111 (2002): 436–45.

19. Hare, Strachan, and Forth, "Psychopathy and Crime" [see chap. 1, n. 4].

20. R. C. Serin, R. D. Peters, and H. E. Barbaree, "Predictors of Psychopathy and Release Outcomes in a Criminal Population," *Psychological Assessment* 2 (1990): 419–22.

21. J. Shine and J. Hobson, "Treatment among Psychopaths Admitted to Prison-Based Therapeutic Community," *Medicine, Science and the Law* 40 (2000): 327–35; J. F. Hemphill, R. D. Hare, and S. Wong, "Psychopathy and Recidivism: A Review," *Legal and Criminological Psychology* 3 (1998): 139–70.

22. J. Hancock, M. Woodworth, and S. Porter, "Hungry Like the Wolf: A Word-Pattern Analysis of the Language of Psychopaths," *Legal and Criminological Psychology*, accessed November 10, 2011, doi:10.1111/j. 2044-8333.2011.02025.x.

23. E. Forouzon and D. J. Cooke, "Figuring Out *la Femme Fatale:* Conceptual and Assessment Issues Concerning Psychopathy in Females," *Behavioral Sciences and the Law* 23 (2005): 765–78.

24. World Health Organization, *The ICD-10 Classification of Mental and Behavioral Disorders* (Geneva: World Health Organization, 1993). www.who.int/classifications/icd/en/GRNBOOK.pdf.

25. S. D. Hart, D. N. Cox, and R. D. Hare, *The Hare PCL: SV—Psychopathy Checklist: Screening Version* (North Tonawanda, NY: Multi-Health Systems, Inc., 1995). Hare's concept of psychopathy was originally made up of two main components or "factors." Factor I related to the emotional and interpersonal components of psychopathy. Factor II contained traits and behaviors that indicate social deviance. Further studies on the PCL–R have stimulated suggestions for reanalysis that would look at three or four, rather than two, factors to define psychopathy. [For a discussion of these studies, see D. J. Cooke and C. Michie, "Refining the Construct of Psychopathy: Towards a Hierarchical Model," *Psychological Assessment* 13, no. 2 (2001): 171–88; K. M. Williams, D. L. Paulhus, and R. D. Hare, "Capturing the Four-Factor Structure of Psychopathy in College Students via Self-Report," *Journal of Personality Assessment* 88 (2007): 205–19.] Hare's current conceptualization of four factors—1a, 1b, 2a, and 2b—still track the original two-factor model. Factors 1a and 1b relate to the core personality features of psychopathy. Factors 2a and 2b encompass the antisocial/criminal characteristics.

The PCL–R was initially validated only in adult male forensic populations, that is, adult men who are in pretrial detention, forensic psychiatric hospitals, and correctional institutions, and the PCL–R manual indicates that it should only be used in those populations. However, subsequent research has supported its use with women and in nonforensic settings. Multiple studies have shown a positive correlation between scores on the PCL–R and the risk of reoffending, violating parole or probation, and reincarceration of convicted offenders. In other words, those who score in the upper range are at higher risk than those with lower scores.

Chapter 3: The Almost Psychopath

26. S. Gustafson and D. Ritzer, "The Dark Side of Normal: A Psychopathy-Linked Pattern Called Aberrant Self-Promotion," *European Journal of Personality* 9 (1995): 147–83; T. Pethman and S. Erlandsson, "Aberrant Self-Promotion or Subclinical Psychopathy in Swedish General Population," *Psychological Record* 52 (2002): 33–50.

27. W. March, *The Bad Seed* (New York: Rinehart, 1954).

Chapter 4: Could It Be Something Else?

28. D. Bear, J. Rosenbaum, and R. Norman, "Aggression in Cat and Human Precipitated by Cholinesterase Inhibitor," *Psychosomatics* 27, no. 7 (1986): 535–36.

29. D. T. Lykken, *The Antisocial Personality Disorders* (Hillsdale, NJ: Lawrence Earlbaum Associates, 1995).

30. "Major Depressive Episode," *Diagnostic and Statistical Manual of Mental Disorders*, 4th ed., text rev. (Washington, DC: American Psychiatric Association, 2000), 349–51.

31. "Narcisstic Personality Disorder," *DSM–IV–TR*, 717.

32. "Borderline Personality Disorder," *DSM–IV–TR*, 710.

33. "Histrionic Personality Disorder," *DSM–IV–TR*, 714.

34. E. L. Barrett, K. L. Mills, and M. Teesson, "Hurt People Who Hurt People: Violence amongst Individuals with Comorbid Substance Use Disorder and Post Traumatic Stress Disorder," *Addictive Behaviors* 36, no. 7 (2011): 721–28.

35. P. Malloy, A. Bihrle, and J. Duffy, "The Orbitofrontal Syndrome," *Archives of Clinical Neuropsychology* 8 (1993): 185–201.

36. D. F. Benson and D. Blumer, "Personality Changes with Frontal Lobe Lesions," in *Psychiatric Aspects of Neurological Disease*, eds. D. F. Benson and D. Blumer (New York: Grune & Stratton, 1975), 151–70.

37. "Asperger's Disorder," *DSM–IV–TR*, 80–84.

38. A. P. Jones, F. G. Happeé, F. Gilbert, S. Burnett, and E. Viding, "Feeling, Caring, Knowing: Different Types of Empathy Deficit in Boys with Psychopathic Tendencies and Autism Spectrum Disorders," *Journal of Child Psychology and Psychiatry* 51, no. 11 (2010): 1188–97.

39. K. Gray, A. C. Jenkins, A. S. Heberlein, and D. M. Wegner, "Distortions of Mind Perception in Psychopathology," *Proceedings of the National Academy of Sciences* 118, no. 2 (2011): 477–79.

40. *DSM–IV–TR*, 93–94.

Chapter 5: Living with an Almost Psychopath

41. M. C. Black, K. C. Basile, M. J. Breiding, S. G. Smith, M. L. Walters, M. T. Merrick, J. Chen, and M. R. Stevens, *The National Intimate Partner and Sexual Violence Survey (NISVS): 2010 Summary Report* (Atlanta, GA: National Center for Injury Prevention and Control, Centers for Disease Control and Prevention, 2011).

42. A. Holtzworth-Munroe, "Male versus Female Intimate Partner Violence: Putting Controversial Findings into Context," *Journal of Marriage and Family* 67 (2005): 1120–25.

43. M. Bhandari, S. Sprague, S. Dosanjh, B. Petrisor, S. Resendes, K. Madden, E. H. Schemitsch, and P.R.A.I.S.E. Investigators, "The Prevalence of Intimate Partner Violence across Orthopedic Fracture Clinics in Ontario," *Journal of Bone and Joint Surgery* 93, no. 2 (2011): 132–41. This study found that those who screened for IPV spanned all ages, ethnicities, and income levels. The study's authors had a female study coordinator screen all women who went to two participating orthopedic centers (both in Ontario). Some patients came directly from emergency rooms, others for follow-up appointments after having been seen for injury. Those who came because of chronic conditions like arthritis were not invited to participate. To ensure that all patients could answer questions privately, the study included only those who came alone or who were able to separate from whomever had accompanied them to the clinics.

44. G. T. Harris, N. Z. Hilton, and M. E. Rice, "Explaining the Frequency of Intimate Partner Violence by Male Perpetrators: Do Attitude, Relationship, and Neighborhood Variables Add to Antisociality?," *Criminal Justice and Behavior* 38, no. 4 (2011): 309–31.

45. M. L. Benson, G. L. Fox, A. DeMaris, and J. Van Wyk, "Neighborhood Disadvantage, Individual Economic Distress and Violence Against Women in Intimate Relationships," *Journal of Quantitative Criminology* 19 (2003): 207–35.

46. K. M. Williams, A. Spidel, and D. L. Paulhus, "Sex, Lies and More Lies: Exploring the Intimate Relationships of Subclinical Psychopaths presented at the first conference of the Society for the Scientific Study of Psychopathy (Vancouver, 2005).

47. M. P. Johnson, "Patriarchal Terrorism and Common Couple Violence: Two Forms of Violence Against Women," *Journal of Marriage and the Family* 57 (1995): 283–94.

48. E. Jacques, "Death and the Mid-Life Crisis," *International Journal of Psychoanalysis* 46 (1965): 502–14.

49. D. J. Levinson, with C. N. Darrow, E. B. Klein, M. H. Levinson, and B. McKee, *The Seasons of a Man's Life* (New York: Ballantine Books, 1978).

50. A. Holtzworth-Munroe and G. L. Stuart, "Typologies of Male Batterers: Three Subtypes and the Differences Among Them," *Psychological Bulletin* 116 (1994): 476–97.

51. Ibid.

52. R. Johnson, E. Gilchrist, A. R. Beech, S. Weston, R. Takriti, and R. Freeman, "A Psychometric Typology of U.K. Domestic Violence Offenders," *Journal of Interpersonal Violence* 21, no. 10 (2006): 1270–85.

53. M. K. Ehrensaft, P. Cohen, J. Brown, E. Smailes, H. Chen, and J. G. Johnson, "Intergenerational Transmission of Partner Violence: A 20-Year Prospective Study," *Journal of Consulting and Clinical Psychology* 71 (2003): 741–53.

54. L. K. Hamberger, J. M. Lohr, D. Bonge, and D. F. Tolin, "An Empirical Classification of Motivations for Domestic Violence," *Violence Against Women* 3, no. 4 (1996): 401–23.

55. E. W. Gondolf, "The Weak Evidence for Batterer Program Alternatives," *Aggression and Violent Behavior* 16 (2011): 347–53.

56. Dunlop et al., "The Effects of Sertraline on Psychopathic Traits."

Chapter 6: Recognizing Almost Psychopathic Traits in Children

57. D. Seagrave and T. Grisso, "Adolescent Development and the Measurement of Juvenile Psychopathy," *Law and Human Behavior* 26 (2002): 219–39; G. M. Vincent and S. D. Hart, "Psychopathy in Childhood and Adolescence: Implications for the Assessment and Management of Multi-Problem Youths," in *Multi-Problem Violent Youths: A Foundation for Comparative Research on Needs, Interventions, and Outcomes*, eds. R. R. Corrado, R. Coesch, S. D. Hart, and J. K. Gierowski (Amsterdam: IOS Press, 2002), 150–63.

58. C. E. Izzard, *Human Emotions* (New York: Plenum Press, 1977); C. E. Izzard and P. Harris, "Emotional Development and Developmental Psychopathology," in *Developmental Psychopathology, Vol. 2: Risk, Disorder, and Adaptation*, eds. D. Cicchetti and D. J. Cohen (New York: Wiley, 1995), 467–503.

59. K. R. Cruise, "Measurement of Adolescent Psychopathy: Construct and Predictive Validity in Two Samples of Juvenile Offenders," (PhD diss., University of North Texas, 2000); R. T. Salekin, A. R. Leistico, K. K. Trobst, C. L. Schrum, and J. E. Lochman, "Adolescent Psychopathy and Personality Theory—The Interpersonal Circumplex: Expanding Evidence of a Nomological Net," *Journal of Abnormal Child Psychology* 33 (2005): 445–60.

60. M. R. Dadds, J. Jambrak, D. Pasalich, D. J. Hawes, and J. Brennan, "Impaired Attention to the Eyes of Attachment Figures and the Developmental Origins of Psychopathy," *Journal of Child Psychology and Psychiatry* 52, no. 3 (2011): 238–45.

61. S. Bezdjian, A. Raine, L. A. Baker, and D. R. Lynam, "Psychopathic Personality in Children: Genetic and Environmental Contributions," *Psychological Medicine* 41 (2011): 589–600.

62. Ibid., p. 597.

63. K. M. Williams, C. Nathanson, and D. L. Paulhus, "Identifying and Profiling Scholastic Cheaters: Their Personality, Cognitive Ability, and Motivation," *Journal of Experimental Psychology: Applied* 16, no. 3 (2010): 293–307.

64. P. Sylvers, K. E. Landfield, and S. O. Lilienfeld, "Heavy Episodic Drinking in College Students: Association with Features of Psychopathy and Antisocial Personality Disorder," *Journal of American College Health* 59, no. 5 (2011): 367–72.

65. H. Chabrol, N. van Leeuwen, R. F. Rodgers, and J. C. Gibbs, "Relations between Self-Serving Cognitive Distortions, Psychopathic Traits, and Antisocial Behavior in a Non-Clinical Sample of Adolescents," *Personality and Individual Differences* 51, no. 8 (2011): 887–92.

Chapter 7: Working with an Almost Psychopath

66. S. M. Louth, R. D. Hare, and W. Linden, "Psychopathy and Alexithmia in Female Offenders," *Canadian Journal of Behavioural Science* 30 (1998): 91–98.

67. J. I. Warren, M. L. Burnette, S. C. South, P. Chauhan, R. Bale, R. Friend, and I. Van Patten,"Psychopathy in Women: Structural Modeling and Comorbidity," *International Journal of Law and Psychiatry* 26 (2003): 223–42; J. E. Vitale, S. S. Smith, C. A. Brinkley, and J. P. Newman, "The Reliability and Validity of the Psychopath Checklist–Revised in a Sample of Female Offenders," *Criminal Justice and Behavior* 27 (2002): 541–58.

68. P. Silverthorn, P. J. Frick, and R. Reynolds, "Timing of Onset and Correlates of Severe Problems in Adjudicated Girls and Boys," *Journal of Psychopathology and Behavioral Assessment* 23 (2001): 171–81; P. Silverthorn and P. J. Frick, "Developmental Pathways to Antisocial Behavior: The Delayed Onset Pathway in Girls," *Development and Psychopathology* 11 (1999): 101–26.

69. J. Ronson, *The Psychopath Test* (New York: Riverhead Books, 2011).

70. B. J. Board and K. F. Fritzon, "Disordered Personalities at Work," *Psychology, Crime and Law* 11 (2005): 17–32.

71. Ibid.

72. Workplace Bullying Institute, Gary Namie, research director, "The WBI U.S. Workplace Bullying Survey 2010," conducted by Zogby International, Workplace Bullying Institute, www.workplacebullying.org.

73. S. Mullins-Sweatt, N. G. Glover, K. J. Derefinko, J. D. Miller, and T. A. Widiger, "The Search for the Successful Psychopath," *Journal of Research in Personality* 44, no. 4 (2010): 554–58.

Chapter 8: Confronting Child Abuse by Almost Psychopaths

74. *DSM–IV–TR*, 572.

75. M. C. Seto, J. M. Cantor, and R. Blanchard, "Child Pornography Offenses Are a Valid Diagnostic Indicator of Pedophilia," *Journal of Abnormal Psychology* 115 (2006): 610–15.

76. M. C. Seto, "Pedophilia," *Annual Review of Clinical Psychology* 5 (2009): 391–407.

77. M. C. Seto, *Pedophilia and Sexual Offending Against Children: Theory, Assessment, and Intervention* (Washington, DC: American Psychological Association, 2008).

78. Y. M. Fernandez and W. L. Marshall, "Victim Empathy, Social Self-Esteem, and Psychopathy in Rapists," *Sex Abuse: A Journal of Research and Treatment* 15, no. 1 (2003): 11–26.

79. K. Franklin, "Hebephilia: Quintessence of Diagnostic Pretextuality," *Behavioral Sciences and the Law* 28 (2010): 751–68.

80. R. K. Hanson, A. Gordon, A. J. Harris, J. K. Marques, W. Murphy, V. L. Quinsey, and M. C. Seto, "First Report of the Collaborative Outcome Data Project on the Effectiveness of Psychological Treatment for Sex Offenders," *Sexual Abuse: A Journal of Research and Treatment* 14.2 (2002): 169–94.

Chapter 9: Adults as Victims

81. R. Kaplan, "The Clinicide Phenomenon: An Exploration of Medical Murder," *Australas Psychiatry* 15, no. 4 (2007): 299–304.

Chapter 10: Sick or Slick?

82. *DSM–IV–TR*, 739.

83. K. Dornstein, *Accidentally, on Purpose: The Making of a Personal Injury Underworld in America* (New York: St. Martin's Press, 1996).

84. W. Bogdanich, "A Disability Epidemic among a Railroad's Retirees," *New York Times*, September 20, 2008. Accessed October 27, 2011. www.nytimes.com/2008/09/21/nyregion/21lirr.html?pagewanted=all.

85. Wiley Mittenberg, C. Patton, E. M. Canyock, and D. Condit, "Base Rates of Malingering and Symptom Exaggeration," *Journal of Clinical and Experimental Neuropsychology* 24, no. 8 (2002): 1094–102.

86. G. J. Larrabee, "Detection of Malingering Using Atypical Performance Patterns on Standard Neuropsychological Tests," *Clinical Neuropsychology* 17, no. 3 (2003): 410–25.

87. K. W. Greve, J. S. Ord, K. J. Bianchini, and K. L. Curtis, "Prevalence of Malingering in Patients with Chronic Pain Referred for Psychologic Evaluation in a Medico-Legal Context," *Archives of Physical Medicine and Rehabilitation* 90, no. 7 (2009): 1117–26.

88. M. Rohling, L. Binder, and J. Langhinrichsen-Rohling, "Money Matters: A Meta-Analytic Review of the Association between Financial Compensation and the Experience and Treatment of Chronic Pain," *Health Psychology* 14, no. 10 (1995): 537–47.

89. Workers' Compensation Anti-Fraud Activity: Survey Results (Minnesota Department of Labor and Industry: State, 1995).

90. G. W. Stevens, J. K. Deuling, and A. A. Armenakis, "Successful Psychopaths: Are They Unethical Decision-Makers and Why?," *Journal of Business Ethics*, July 12, 2011. Accessed October 28, 2011. www.springerlink.com/content/4g885w8142011640/.

91. J. C. Huffman and T. A. Stern, "The Diagnosis and Treatment of Munchausen's Syndrome," *General Hospital Psychiatry* 25 (2003): 358–63.

Chapter 11: What to Do When You Find Yourself in Almost Psychopath Territory

92. J. Maltby, A. M. Wood, L. Day, T. W. H. Kon, A. Colley, and P. A. Linley, "Personality Predictors of Levels of Forgiveness Two and a Half Years after the Transgression," *Journal of Research in Personality* 42 (2008): 1088–94; M. C. Whited, A. L. Wheat, and K. T. Larkin, "The Influence of Forgiveness and Apology on Cardiovascular Reactivity and Recovery in Response to Mental Stress," *Journal of Behavioral Medicine* 33, no. 4 (2010): 293–304; J. R. Webb, L. Toussaint, C. Z. Kalpakjian, and D. G. Tate, "Forgiveness and Health-Related Outcomes among People with Spinal Cord Injury," *Disability and Rehabilitation* 32, no. 5 (2010): 360–66.

about the authors

Ronald Schouten, MD, JD, is an associate professor of psychiatry at Harvard Medical School and director of the Law & Psychiatry Service at Massachusetts General Hospital. In addition to his clinical practice, he has served as a consultant to corporations and government agencies on subjects including occupational mental health, workplace and campus violence, insider threats, and terrorism. He has served as an expert witness in criminal and civil cases. A graduate of Haverford College, he earned his juris doctor degree at Boston University, practiced law in Chicago, and then obtained his medical degree at the University of Illinois in Chicago.

James Silver, JD, is a former Assistant United States Attorney and current criminal defense lawyer who has tried cases and argued appeals on offenses ranging from shoplifting to first-degree murder. He was also a civil litigator at one of the nation's largest law firms. He is a graduate of the University of Notre Dame and Harvard Law School.

· ◆ ·

Hazelden, a national nonprofit organization founded in 1949, helps people reclaim their lives from the disease of addiction. Built on decades of knowledge and experience, Hazelden offers a comprehensive approach to addiction that addresses the full range of patient, family, and professional needs, including treatment and continuing care for youth and adults, research, higher learning, public education and advocacy, and publishing.

A life of recovery is lived "one day at a time." Hazelden publications, both educational and inspirational, support and strengthen lifelong recovery. In 1954, Hazelden published *Twenty-Four Hours a Day*, the first daily meditation book for recovering alcoholics, and Hazelden continues to publish works to inspire and guide individuals in treatment and recovery, and their loved ones. Professionals who work to prevent and treat addiction also turn to Hazelden for evidence-based curricula, informational materials, and videos for use in schools, treatment programs, and correctional programs.

Through published works, Hazelden extends the reach of hope, encouragement, help, and support to individuals, families, and communities affected by addiction and related issues.

For questions about Hazelden publications,
please call **800-328-9000** or visit us online
at **hazelden.org/bookstore.**